Fires in the Mirror

Acclaim for Anna Deavere Smith and *Fires in the Mirror*

"I've seen nothing smarter, more engaging and entertaining in recent theater. Anna Deavere Smith is one of the few who are still creating for the theater. She's a fine example of a contemporary Brechtian in the sense that she never wholly loses herself in the characters. You always see the talented choice-making artist peeping through."

—Spalding Gray

"Smith turns the headlines into pure drama."

—*New York Daily News*

"A most fascinating play...a tour de force...not only potent social commentary in search of truth, but also a poignant look at a glaring culture gap."

—*Hollywood Reporter*

"Spellbinding. Deeply perceptive. Provocative. Throbs with understandable emotions on all sides."

—*New York Newsday*

"You could describe Ms. Smith as a documentary film maker who has simply decided to dispense with the camera. *Fires in the Mirror* couldn't be more timely. Yet the timelessness of the piece is what impressed me."

—David Richards, *New York Times*

"An extraordinary play...riveting...an unsparing rendering of the myriad emotions of the [Crown Heights] incident—not just the rage that hit the headlines but also the bitterness, grief and bewilderment that touched the community."

—*Wall Street Journal*

Anna Deavere Smith

with a foreword by Cornel West

Fires in the Mirror

Crown Heights, Brooklyn and Other Identities

Anchor Books
Doubleday
New York London
Toronto Sydney
Auckland

This book is dedicated to the residents of
Crown Heights, Brooklyn, and to the memory of
Gavin Cato and Yankel Rosenbaum

Contents

Acknowledgments   xiii

Foreword
   Cornel West   xvii

Introduction   xxiii

The Crown Heights Conflict:
   Background Information   xliii

Crown Heights, Brooklyn
   A Chronology   xlvii

The Characters   lv

Production History   lix

Fires in the Mirror

Identity

Ntozake Shange	The Desert	3
Anonymous Lubavitcher Woman	Static	5
George C. Wolfe	101 Dalmations	9

Mirrors

| Aaron M. Bernstein | Mirrors and Distortions | 13 |

Hair

Anonymous Girl	Look in the Mirror	16
The Reverend Al Sharpton	Me and James's Thing	19
Rivkah Siegal	Wigs	23

Race

Angela Davis   **Rope**   **27**

Rhythm

Monique "Big Mo" Matthews   **Rhythm and Poetry**   **35**

Seven Verses

Leonard Jeffries   **Roots**   **40**

Letty Cottin Pogrebin   **Near Enough to Reach**   **50**

Minister Conrad Mohammed   **Seven Verses**   **52**

Letty Cottin Pogrebin   **Isaac**   **59**

Robert Sherman   **Lousy Language**   **63**

Crown Heights, Brooklyn, August 1991

Rabbi Joseph Spielman   **No Blood in His Feet**   **67**

The Reverend Canon Doctor
   Heron Sam   **Mexican Standoff**   **74**

Anonymous Young Man #1   **Wa Wa Wa**   **79**

Michael S. Miller   **"Heil Hitler"**   **85**

Henry Rice   **Knew How to Use Certain Words**   **88**

Norman Rosenbaum   **My Brother's Blood**   **94**

Norman Rosenbaum   **Sixteen Hours Difference**   **97**

Anonymous Young Man #2   **Bad Boy**   **100**

Sonny Carson   **Chords**   **103**

Rabbi Shea Hecht   **Ovens**   **109**

The Reverend Al Sharpton   **Rain**   **113**

Richard Green   **Rage**   **117**

Roslyn Malamud   **The Coup**   **122**

Reuven Ostrov   **Pogroms**   **129**

Carmel Cato   **Lingering**   **135**

Acknowledgments

For invaluable creative assistance: George C. Wolfe, Joanne Akalaitis, Merry Conway, Bonita Bradley, Thulani Davis, Deborah Hecht, Robert Williams, Kristin Linklater, Luly Santangelo, and Juanita Rice.

The New York Shakespeare Festival, Rosemarie Tichler, Jason Steven Cohen, James Morrison, Bruce Campbell, and Cary Wong, for institutional support and more.

The Bunting Institute, Florence Ladd, and Barbara Johnson, without whose support *Fires in the Mirror* could never have been written.

The Stanford University Department of Drama, Michael Ramsaur; and Deans Ewart Thomas and Carolyn Lougee, the School of Humanities, and the Committee for Black Performing Arts at Stanford, for supporting my fellowship year at the Bunting Institute.

Cathy Clark and Mary Forcade at the Bay Area Playwrights Festival '91, for the work they did with me while I was writing *Identities, Mirrors and Distortions*, which provided the first structure for *Fires in the Mirror.*

Lindsay Law and "American Playhouse" for making the show more accessible to the general public and Cherie Fortis for vigilant and sensitive producing.

The Ford and Revson Foundations for their outreach support for the televised version of *Fires in the Mirror*.

For research: Paula Cerrone.

For friendship, mentorship, and discussion throughout the development of the "On the Road" series:

Donald Bogle, Roberta Goodman, Glenn Young, Joy

Carlin, Ted Hoffman, Denise Nicholas, Irene Mecchi, Blair Fuller, Peter and Carol Mack, John Emigh, Paula Vogel, Tania Modleski, Valerie Smith, Richard Yarborough, Jane Robinson, Michael Maynard, Kathy and Peter Leech, Tony Newfield, Randy Morey, David Terry, Hilda Silverman, Pat Kaufman, Sydne Mahone, Martha Jones, and Rhonda Blair.

For their hard work, inventiveness, creativity, and participation in experiments, exercises, and productions related to the exploration of language, character, and difference:

Pamela Putch, Maggie Jakobson, Jessica Schanberg, Joseph Phillips, Tamara Tunie, Lori Lowe, Joe Siracusa, Susan Dibble, Pricilla Shanks, Maryanna Austin, Taman Aseff, Lamont Johnson, Alex Thomas, Leah Tewles, Richard Harrison, Omar Wasow, Anna Scott, Bridgit Evans, Jane Lin, Alice Wu, Aleeta Hayes, Christina Rouner, Brett Heller, Gita Srinivasan, Kevin Stein, Theresa Player, Erica Nashan, Phillip Safley, and all of the actors and students who have worked with me, especially those I taught at Carnegie Mellon University, 1979–80; those in the first "On the Road," in New York City, 1983; those at the American Conservatory Theatre during the summers of 1986, 1988, and 1989; and those at Stanford University, 1990–91.

For assistance: Jilchristina Vest.

For their generosity and suggestions in Crown Heights: Robert Sherman, of the Increase the Peace Corps, City of New York; David Lazerson, Richard Green, and Henry Rice.

For inspiration:

Ricardo Kahn and the Crossroads Theatre Company; Tania Leon; Judith Jamison; Adrienne Kennedy and her play *A Movie Star Has to Star in Black and White*, which dramatically changed my perception of the relationship of language to character; Ntozake Shange for what her presence has done to redefine the position of Black women in American theatre; Peter Zeisler; Charlayne Hunter-Gault, one of my first interviewees, and for the only text that I performed in nearly every "On the Road" until *Fires in the Mirror*; Mr. and Mrs. Deaver Young Smith, Jr.

Finally, I acknowledge Esther Blake, Jane Kennedy, Marcel Fieve, Eric Jazman, Marilyn Saviola, Meredith Monk, Homi Bhabha, Guillermo Gomez Pena, and *all* those who have granted me interviews, and for the beautiful, remarkable, unique ways that they speak.

Foreword
Cornel West

The contemporary Black-Jewish dialogue suffers from three basic shortcomings. First, we often appeal to an abstract humanism and faceless universalism that refuse to confront the concrete conflicts that divide us. Second, we usually conduct the conversation as if the tensions between Black and Jewish *men* are exactly the same as those between Black and Jewish *women*. Third, we attempt to conduct the exchange in a public space equally appealing to both Blacks and Jews—yet fail to recognize that Jews seem to be much more eager to inhabit this public space than Blacks.

Anna Deavere Smith's powerful work, *Fires in the Mirror*, is the most significant artistic exploration of Black-Jewish relations in our time, precisely because she takes us beyond the three basic shortcomings. In the midst of the heated moment of murder, mayhem, and madness of the Crown Heights crisis, she gives us poignant portraits of the everyday human faces that get caught up in the situation. Her sensitive renderings of the tragic and comic aspects of the reactions and responses of Blacks and Jews to the Crown Heights crisis give our universal moral principles a particular heartfelt empathy. Her ability to move our passions, not only takes us beyond any self-righteous condescension toward parochial Hasidism and provincial Black urbanites, but also forces us to examine critically our own complicity in cultural stereotypes that imprison our imaginations and thereby make *us* parochial and provincial. In the best tradition of tragedy, Smith explores the possibilities of human choices in an urgent crisis that yields limited options. Not to choose "sides" is itself a choice—yet to view the crisis as simply and solely a matter of choosing sides is to reduce the history and complexity of the crisis in a vulgar Manichean manner. In the best tradition of comedy, Smith exposes the ordinary foibles of human responses to this serious crisis, which signify our own imperfect and tension-ridden views about the Crown Heights episode. Her funny characterizations—that for some border on caricatures—provoke genuine laughter even as we know that laughter is an inadequate response to the pain, cruelty, and sheer absurdity of the crisis. We laugh, not only because her characters are in some fundamental ways like us—human-all-too-human; but also because we refuse to give pain, cruelty, and absurdity the last word. Once again, *Fires in the Mirror* is testimony to how art can take us beyond ourselves as we examine ourselves even in an ugly moment of xenophobic frenzy.

For too long the Black-Jewish dialogue has been cast in masculine terms by principally male interlocutors. Is it no accident that the major issues of contention—Affirmative Action and the security of the state of Israel—tend to highlight the power struggles of men in the public spaces of jobs and the military? Smith explodes this narrow framework by taking us into the private spheres of American society where the complex discourses of women often take place in patriarchal America. This is especially so in Hasidic and Black America where the access of women to public space—especially major leadership roles—is frowned upon. Yet Smith neither romanticizes nor idealizes Hasidic, Black, or secular Jewish women. Instead, she humanizes the Black-Jewish dialogue by including the diverse and often conflicting voices within Black and Jewish America. This kind of polyphony of perspectives is rarely aired and heard in the Black-Jewish dialogue. It should not surprise us that most Jewish women are less disposed to oppose Affirmative Action than many Jewish men, that strong Jewish women's voices are heard in the Peace Now movement in Israel, or that Black women's critiques of Black nationalist Sonny Carson are persuasive. In short, the gendered character of the Black-Jewish dialogue often produces obstacles that compound the problems and render us more paralyzed. Smith's deepening of this dialogue by *de-patriarchalizing* our conversation is a major contribution in this regard.

Fires in the Mirror is a grand example of how art can constitute a public space that is perceived by people as empowering rather than disempowering. What I mean by this is that many Blacks are deeply suspicious—or even downright pessimistic—about entering a Black-Jewish dialogue. This is especially so for young Black people who are reluctant to engage with Jews who often perceive themselves as underdogs yet who usually are middle-class Americans. This issue of Jews as victims in an American context unsettles many African Americans. Needless to say, the Jewish experience in America is quite atypical in Jewish history. Yet, for many Black people, the Jewish experience in America is *the* Jewish experience that counts most in the present situation. And since the Black experience in America is much worse than the Jewish experience in America, the notion of two oppressed groups in America coming together for dialogue smacks of a dishonesty and even a diversion.

And, to complicate the situation even more, the degradation of the public sphere by conservative elites in the past two decades has exacerbated distrust between any group or constituency—especially progressive ones. This degradation has principally taken the form of associating the public sphere with the faults of Black people. For example, public housing, public education, and even public transportation are associated in the American mind with the faults of Black people. Is it not the case that the very mention of public provisions—not tax breaks nor subsidies for corporate America but subsistence support— evokes images of lazy Black men and welfare queens? The political success of playing this insidious racial card has led to a large-scale gutting of public life that has yielded a balkanized populace with little sense of public-mindedness and a narrow obsession with one's constituency and identity. If one cannot trust people as citizens in the public sphere one must close ranks and trust only those in one's tribe, and tribal strife in America is usually racial in content.

In Black America, this tribal mentality has often focused on those who are the public face of the larger system. The relatively invisible WASP corporate and bank elites are rarely targeted since they are so far removed from the everyday life of Black people. Instead, the most visible beneficiaries of Black consumption, e.g., shop owners and landlords in Black communities, or the most vociferous critics of Black strategies for progress, e.g., conservative opponents of Affirmative Action, loom large as objects of Black rage.

In Jewish America, this tribal mentality has often highlighted those who make the loudest noise about Jewish conspiracy and Jewish control. The relatively quiet, covert anti-Semites in high places in American life tend to receive more genteel treatment, while the most vocal anti-Semites garner the bulk of Jewish rage.

In this scenario, WASP corporate and bank elites receive little attention regarding how they promote policies and programs that contribute to Black poverty, and covert anti-Semitic elites get off relatively scot-free in regard to maintaining impediments to Jewish mobility. And since the public sphere is racialized, any entry of Black people in a public dialogue often means that they—we— are on the defensive. So Black people must give an account of our faults, condemn some of our xenophobic spokespersons, explain the "silence" of Black moral voices, et cetera. This sense of Black people having to do much of the "work" and bear most of the burden in public dialogues generates a deep distrust of any such public dialogue for many Black people. Furthermore, any hint of a double standard at work in such a public dialogue spoils the conversation. This is why those Black people who do enter public dialogues are eager to hear the faults, e.g., xenophobia, of other communities as well as that of Black communities.

Smith's *Fires in the Mirror* is not only aware of this

delicate set of issues but also responds to them with the kind of risk and sensitivity that sets Black people at ease. She lets Black people know that a fair treatment of all our faults will transpire—so we can confront, examine, parody, and maybe begin to overcome these faults. And she is keenly aware that these activities will never get off the ground without a clearing of the air so that bonds of trust can be forged.

As a citizen, Smith knows that there can be no grappling with Black anti-Semitism and Jewish anti-Black racism without a vital public sphere and that there can be no vital public sphere without genuine bonds of trust. As an artist, she knows that public performance has a unique capacity to bring us together—to take us out of our tribal mentalities—for self-critical examination and artistic pleasure. *Fires in the Mirror* is one sure sign, an oasis of hope, that human art can triumph in the face of a frightening urban crisis—a crisis symptomatic of a national tragedy. It provides us with a glimpse of what we need and what we must do if we are ever to overcome the xenophobic cancer that threatens to devour the soul of the precious yet precarious democratic experiment called America.

Introduction

Fires in the Mirror is a part of a series of theater (or performance) pieces called On the Road: A Search for American Character, which I create by interviewing people and later performing them using their own words. My goal has been to find American character in the ways that people speak. When I started this project, in the early 1980s, my simple introduction to anyone I interviewed was, "If you give me an hour of your time, I'll invite you to see yourself performed." At that time I was not as interested in performance or in social commentary as I was in experimenting with language and its relationship to character.

I was trained as an actress in a conservatory, which at the time placed emphasis on classical training. On the Road is about contemporary life. It's ironic that it was inspired by classical training. Words have always held a particular power for me. I remember leafing through a book of Native American poems one morning while I was waiting for my Shakespeare class to begin and being struck by a phrase from the preface, "The word, the word above all, is truly magical, not only by its meaning, but by its artful manipulation."

This quote, which I added to my journal, reminded me of something my grandfather had told me when I was a girl: "If you say a word often enough it becomes your own." I added that phrase to my journal next to the quote about the magic of words. When I traveled home to Baltimore for my grandfather's funeral a year after my journal entry, I mentioned my grandfather's words to my father. He corrected me. He told me that my grandfather had actually said, "If you say a word often enough, it *becomes* you." I was still a student at the time, but I knew even then, even before I had made a conscious decision to teach as well as act, that my grandfather's words would be important.

I began a series of conversations with my Shakespeare teacher, Juanita Rice, who was brilliant and inspiring. In the first class she talked about speech as an action. She asked us to consider speech in Shakespeare as thought and stressed the importance of thinking on the word, rather than between the words in order to discover the character. She told us to take any fourteen lines of Shakespeare and to repeat the passage over and over again until something happened. No thinking. Just speaking. I chose a speech of Queen Margaret's from Richard III. The Queen says to the Duchess of York:

> From forth the kennel of thy womb hath crept
> A hell hound that doth hunt us all to death
> That dog that had its teeth before his eyes
> To worry lambs and lap their gentle blood
> That foul defacer of God's handiwork
> That excellent grand tyrant of the earth
> That reigns in galled eyes of weeping souls
> Thy womb let loose to chase us to our graves.

I followed Juanita's instructions, saying the fourteen lines over and over well into the wee hours of the morning. I didn't know enough at the time about Queen Margaret, or about Shakespeare to realize that what I had been repeating was very strong language, which was bound to evoke powerful images. In one evening I had traveled to a very dark and decadent world. The speed with which this happened had everything to do with the power of the words. It had everything to do with how the words themselves had worked on *me. I had not controlled the words. I had presented myself as an empty vessel, a repeater, and they had shown their power.* I was soon to learn about the power of rhythm and imagery to evoke the spirit of a character, of a play, of a time.

I then started thinking that if I listened carefully to people's words, and particularly to their rhythms, that I could use language to learn about my own time. If I could find a way to really inhabit the words of those around me, like I had inhabited those of Queen Margaret, that I could learn about the spirit, the imagination, and the challenges of my own time, firsthand.

Actors are very impressionable people, or some would say, suggestible people. We are trained to develop aspects of our memories that are more emotional and sensory than intellectual. The general public often wonders how actors remember their lines. What's more remarkable to me, is how actors remember, recall, and reiterate feelings and sensations. The body has a memory just as the mind does. The heart has a memory, just as the mind does. The act of speech is a physical act. It is powerful enough that it can create, with the rest of the body, a kind of cooperative dance. That dance is a sketch of something that is inside a person, and not fully revealed by the words alone. I came to realize that if I were able to record part of the dance—that is, the spoken part—and reenact it, the rest of the body would follow. I could then create the illusion of being another person by reenacting something they had said *as they had said it*. Using my grandfather's idea that if I said a word often enough it would *become* me, the reenactment, or the reiteration of a person's words would also teach me about that person.

I had been trained in the tradition of acting called "psychological realism." A basic tenet of psychological realism is that characters live inside of you and that you create a character through a process of realizing your own similarity to the character. When I later became a teacher of acting, I began to become more and more troubled by the self-oriented method. I began to look for ways to engage my students in putting themselves in other people's shoes. This went against the grain of the tradition, which was to get the character to walk in the *actor's shoes*. It became less and less interesting intellectually to bring the dramatic literature of the world into a classroom of people in their late teens and twenties, and to explore it within the framework of their real lives. Aesthetically it seemed limited, because most of the times the characters all sounded the same. Most characters spoke somewhere inside the rhythmic range of the students. More troubling was that this method left an important bridge out of acting. The spirit of acting is the *travel* from the self to the other. This "self-based" method seemed to come to a spiritual halt. It saw the self as the ultimate home of the character. To me, the search for character is constantly in motion. It is a quest that moves back and forth between the self and the other.

I needed evidence that you could find a character's psychological reality by "inhabiting" that character's words. I needed evidence of the limitations of basing a character on a series of metaphors from an actor's real life. I wanted to develop an alternative to the self-based technique, a technique that would begin with the other and come to the self, a technique that would empower the other to find the actor rather than the other way around. I needed very graphic evidence that the manner of speech could be a mark of individuality. If we were to inhabit the speech pattern of another, and walk in the speech of another, we could find the individuality of the other and experience that individuality viscerally. I became increasingly convinced that the activity of reenactment could tell us as much, if not more, about another individual than the process of learning about the other by using the self as a frame of reference. The frame of reference for the other would *be* the other. Learning about the other by being the other requires the use of all aspects of memory, the memory of the body, mind, and heart, as well as the words.

The last fifteen to twenty years have given the public consciousness an extended vocabulary for the self. This vocabulary fed the popularity of self-oriented techniques. I think that a vocabulary which is at once political, intellectual, sentimental, visceral, and social would bring life to art. The creation of the On the Road project required that I have a way of thinking that involved multiple vocabularies.

Trying to do other-oriented work also raised some questions which may interest the general public. Any of us who engage in extroverted activities are aware of our inhibitions. I am interested in how inhibitions affect our ability to empathize. If I have an inhibition about *acting* like a man, it may also point to an inhibition I have about *seeing* a man or *hearing* a man. To develop a voice one must develop an ear. To complete an action, one must have a clear vision. Does the inability to empathize start with an inhibition, or a reluctance to see? Do racism and prejudice instruct those inhibitions? If I passed out a piece of poetry to be read by a racially mixed group and I asked them to read it with an English accent, most of them would try. If I passed out a piece of Black poetry written in dialect, many would be inhibited and fearful of offending others. In a playwriting class, I gave an exercise called "gang writing." Students were asked to write short scenes about gangs inspired by gang writing. A student raised the question, "Isn't it offensive for us, here in our privileged environment, to write about gangs?" Does privilege mean one shouldn't *see*? At the same time, the standard for excellence is still a Eurocentric theater written by and for white men. Who else can participate? How? Does it mean new plays? Does it mean rethinking old plays? The mirrors of society do not mirror society.

"Who has the right to see what?" "Who has the right to say what?" "Who has the right to speak for whom?" These questions have plagued the contemporary theater. These questions address both issues of employment equity and issues of *who is portrayed*. These questions are the questions that unsettle and prohibit a democratic theater in America. If only a man can speak for a man, a woman for a woman, a Black person for all Black people, then we, once again, inhibit the *spirit* of theater, which lives in the *bridge* that makes unlikely aspects *seem* connected. The bridge doesn't make them the same, it merely *displays* how two unlikely *aspects* are *related*. These relationships of the *unlikely*, these connections of things that don't fit together are crucial to American theater and culture if theater and culture plan to help us assemble our obvious differences. The self-centered technique has taken the bridge out of the process of creating character, it has taken metaphor out of acting. It has made the heart smaller, the spirit less gregarious, and the mind less apt to be able to hold on to contradictions or opposition.

At the time that I began my work, celebrity interviews exploded in popular culture. *Interview* magazine began publication at the very moment that I was beginning to experiment with some of these ideas. There were more television talk shows being produced, and real-life drama seemed to be a definite point of fascination for the public. I watched talk shows, and read print interviews, and eventually started to transcribe the television talk shows, and use them along with print interviews as scripts. I staged many of these interviews, looking for the moment in the interview when the celebrity was struggling with the interviewer to free his or her identity from the perception that the interviewer had.

As an exercise I had my students reenact these celebrity interviews. I was after more than mimicry. I was using the interviews as a structure for the students to become the other. A character from a play does not have a visible identity until the actor creates a body for that character. The self-oriented technique involves rendering characters who looked and acted like the actors. What are the subtleties in real-life behavior that could be used in the creation of characters? There are linguistic as well as physical details that make a person unique. My overall goal was to show that no one acts like anyone else. No one speaks like anyone else. Identity, in fact, lives in the unique way that a person departs from the English language in a perfect state to create something that is individual. Ntozake Shange's selection in *Fires in the Mirror* speaks to this: "Identity is . . . it's a way of knowing that no matter where I put myself, that I am not necessarily what's around me. I am a part of my surroundings and I become separate from them, and it's being able to make those differentiations clearly that gives us an identity."

Ultimately I began to conduct my own interviews. Talk shows and print interviews of celebrities were often battles between what the interviewer wanted to pretend to be uncovering and what the subject was willing to reveal. Sometimes the battle was authentic, and sometimes it was that the interviewer and the celebrity were in cahoots to give the illusion that something new was on the brink of being uncovered. In fact, it's my experience now that public figures are frequently more difficult to use in my work, because it is less likely that they will say something that they have never said before. It is fully understandable that people who have a relationship to the media learn their way around an interview. The act of speech, then, does become performance rather than discovery. On the other hand, occasionally, public figures are so expert at this kind of performance that they have a greater gift than actors for making what they have said before seem as though they are saying it for the first time. The Reverend Al Sharpton, in *Fires in the Mirror*, is an example of such a person. He is known as the thirty-second sound-bite king. His performance is so wonderful, however, that many actors would envy his ability to work a crowd. My interview with the Reverend Sharpton lasted little more than fifteen or twenty minutes, but his gifts of communication are so great that the material was as rich as material that I have gotten from people who I spoke with much longer. In other words, regardless of the Reverend Sharpton's sound-bite speech, *he* is completely present in the speech. That kind of presence is a gift.

My goal was to create an atmosphere in which the interviewee would experience his/her own authorship. Speaking teaches us what our natural "literature" is. In fact, everyone, in a given amount of time, will say something that is like poetry. The process of getting to that poetic moment is where "character" lives. If I were to reiterate the person's pursuit of that poetic moment, as well as the poetic moment itself, I could "go into character." The pursuit is frequently filled with *uh*s and *um*s and, in fact, the wrong words, if any words at all, and almost always what would be considered "bad grammar." I suppose much of communication could be narrowed down to "the point." This project is not about a point, it is about a route. It is *on* the road. Character lives in the linguistic road as well as the destination.

In the midst of doing the original experiments with language I became very interested in performing. Some of my students were extremely receptive to this work, and very dedicated. Others didn't see its value, and were very committed to the discovery of themselves. They believed that they couldn't be someone else until they knew themselves. My argument was, and still is, that it doesn't have to be either/or, and that neither comes first. The discovery of human behavior can happen in motion. It can be a process of moving from the self to the other and the other to the self. Nevertheless, my argument didn't always sink in. For example, I arranged to have a student of mine meet a person I had interviewed for her to perform. My student spent the entire evening talking about herself. Ideally, she would have used the time to listen and learn everything she could about the woman she was going to portray. This actor, like others I worked with, was actually awkward when meeting the people she would later portray and frightened to have them come to the performance. Was her talking about herself to her subject a declaration of her own identity? Was it a last-ditch effort to say "I am" before saying "You are"?

I decided to abandon the experiment designed for the classroom, and to work out my hypotheses on myself as a performer. I knew that by using another person's language, it was possible to portray what was invisible about that individual. It struck me that this could work on a social level as well as an individual level. Could language also be a photograph of what was unseen about society just as it reflects what is unseen in an individual?

The project took shape during a time that many institutions were going through identity shifts with regard to gender and ethnicity. I had commissions to create pieces in some institutions that were in transformation. One of the people I interviewed early in the process was a Provost at Princeton University, who pointed out to me that there was a tension between the perception of a place, which is frequently embedded in traditions, and the moment-to-moment identity of a place. For me, the battle between those who prefer the perception of a place and those who claim to experience the reality as different from that, was dramatic. This battle adds up to an identity in motion, but a palpable identity nevertheless.

In America, identity is always being negotiated. To what extent do people who come to America have to give up something about their own identity to conform to an idea of what an American is? Crown Heights, Brooklyn, was the most graphic display I had witnessed of the negotiation of identity. No one in Crown Heights looked like a movie-star version of America. This was magnified by the fact that the overall picture of Crown Heights was black and white. The residents were, for the most part, Blacks and Whites. The Hasidim usually wore black and white. Identity was declared visibly. This was no Princeton University, where a Black student, wearing a Princeton jersey might be shocked when a guard stopped him to find out whether or not he belonged there. Everybody seemed to know who they were and how they were seen. Everyone wore their roots on their heads. The Hasidic men wore yarmulkes and black hats, and women wore wigs. The African American and Caribbean Americans frequently had on hats with Afro-centric meaning, or dreadlocks and shells in their hair. The lines were so clearly drawn that at any moment they were ready to snap. The tension was not a tension that was moving an identity forward, it was a tension that threatened to explode. That tension did explode, when a car driven by a member of the entourage of a Jewish religious leader ran up onto a sidewalk and killed one Black child and seriously injured another. In the mist of the steam that blew out of the radiator of that car, twenty Black youths attack a Jewish man and stabbed him. He died in the same hospital where the young boy who had been run over died.

There is an inevitable tension in America. It is the tension of identity in motion, the tension of identity which is in contest with an old idea, but a resonant idea of America. It was developed initially, or so we are told, by men, by White men, but an idea which has in fact, been adapted by women and people of color. Can we guide that tension so that it is, in fact, identity in motion, identity, which like a train can pick up passengers and take them to their destination? Or is this tension always going to be derailed onto a sidewalk where some innocents are waiting to get struck down.

Seven-year-old Gavin Cato and his cousin Angela were playing with a bicycle on a hot summer night. Gavin didn't even know how to ride a bike yet; Angela was teaching him. He was practicing when the car came up on to the sidewalk, smashing him into a wall and knocking down a cement pillar. Some say it was an accident, others call it a murder. To them, the swift motorcade of Rebbe Menachem Schneerson, which crossed that intersection every week, was bound to have killed someone.

They would ask why the Rebbe, with a police escort, was allowed to exceed the speed limit on a city street. To the members of the orthodox Hasidic sect known as the Lubavitchers, this treatment was taken for granted; the Rebbe was, after all, their spiritual leader. To the Black people who lived in the neighborhood, his traveling in an entourage was an intrusion; that this intrusion was protected by the police magnified the situation. Yet this story was not as black and white as I had thought. In fact, this story was also about the relationship of the police to the community: The police were seen as pervasive and oppressive by Black people, and often as ineffective and absent by the Lubavitchers.

On many occasions Black people who lived in Crown Heights had gathered to try to stop what they considered the special privileges that the Lubavitchers enjoyed. Whenever there were holidays or times of worship, the street in front of the synagogue was blocked off to traffic. An African American gynecologist who had offices on that street told me that one of his pregnant patients, on her way to see him after her water had broken, couldn't drive up to the office. "What if a woman is bleeding, or her water is broken, and she has to walk? . . . I don't know how far."

The Lubavitchers, who had come here to study and to

worship, were daily feeling more and more vulnerable to the amount of crime around them. And they would ultimately come to believe that the justice system had failed them. Hours after Gavin Cato's death, a young Jewish scholar, Yankel Rosenbaum, was fatally stabbed by a group of young Black men. When the case went to court, the young Caribbean American man accused of the stabbing was acquitted. The city then heard from the Lubavitchers the rhetoric and chanting that had been invoked by African Americans, including the slogan, "No Justice, No Peace." As a rabbi told me when I returned to Crown Heights after the verdict (and after *Fires in the Mirror* had closed in New York), "What the liberals have told us all these years, that the Blacks have their rage, well the Whites are getting it now; it's a two-way street."

On the surface this picture was Black and White. When one looks more closely, one sees something much more interesting than the stark lines of Black and White. One sees motion, and one hears multiple symphonies. The Black people didn't all come from one place, and neither do the Hasidim. One looks closely and one sees that not every hat is the same kind of black hat and not every yarmulke is the same kind of yarmulke. Multiple languages are being spoken. The Lubavitchers who walked along the short block (which came to be my favorite) of Kingston Avenue at Eastern Parkway, were from the Middle East, England, Australia, South Africa. The young Black men I talked to had accents which were a mixture of bold Brooklynese with rap hand gestures, and Caribbean lilts. Motion. Action. People from everywhere.

During the performance of *Fires in the Mirror*, one major concern audiences have voiced is whether or not I am creating caricatures or stereotypes. This concern has been expressed in many different ways. Some Black people would say that I was "easier" on Jewish people. Some Jewish people would say that I'd gone too far. For example, when I interviewed Rabbi Shea Hecht, he had several crisp dollar bills in the pocket of his shirt. The money came from the Grand Rebbe, who regularly gives out new dollar bills. Some people read this as a comment about Jewish people and affluence. There was a similar concern about a sweater I wore for one of the characters I portrayed, Roz Malamud. The costume designer had chosen a very flashy sequined sweater. Some Jewish (and non-Jewish) members of the audience reacted to the sweater by saying it was *perfect*, others felt it was stereotyping Jewish people as affluent. In reality, according to the costumer, the outfit Roz *really* wore was much more flashy and expensive than the sweater. Likewise, there were a few Black people who reacted to the Sharpton "Me and James's Thing" section, by saying, "Why did you have to make a big thing about a Black person's hair?" Others felt that the piece told them something about Sharpton's hair that they *didn't* know, which in a way, *broadened* their idea of Sharpton.

These questions, this uneasiness, are sometimes judgments about performance, but they are also indications of the uneasiness we have about seeing difference displayed. Mimicry is *not* character. Character lives in the obvious gap between the real person and my *attempt* to seem like them. I try to close the gap between us, but I applaud the gap between us. I am willing to display my own *unlikeness*.

Post-play discussions were very important. It is part of the idea behind On the Road to 1) bring people together into the same room (the theater) who would normally not be together, and 2) attract people to the theater who don't usually come to the theater. It was important, then, to hear what people said about the experience and important to have them know more about each other than they could gather from responses. On various occasions there were Black people in the audience who gave verbal feedback during the show, saying things like, "Yes," "All right," "Teach," et cetera. Once I heard a woman saying throughout the show, "Oy." I wish her "Oy" had been in the same audience as a "Teach." When the audience talks, they are talking as much to each other as to me.

There is a gap between the perception of a place and the individuals who are responsible for keeping that perception alive. The individuals inside are frequently fighting that their individual voices be heard, while the walls of the place, which are the mask, and the perception, are reluctant to give over to the voices of the individuals. Those in the margins are always trying to get to the center, and those at the center, frequently in the name of tradition, are trying to keep the margins at a distance. Part of the identity of a place is the tension between those in the margins, and those in the center, and they all live behind the walls which wear the tradition. I have been going to the places where this tension is evident to find American character. Can this tension be productive, or will it explode and in the process kill and maim those who happen to be in the wrong place at the wrong time? How can some of us intervene? My answer to the first question is yes, this tension can be productive, in so far as it causes motion, and that we watch and document that motion. To do that, we have to interest those people around us in motion, in moving from one side to the other, in experiencing one hand and the other hand, and to building bridges *between* places. My answer to the second question is that one kind of intervention is the intervention of listening. We can listen for what is inconsistent as well as for what is consistent. We can listen to what the dominant pattern of speech is, and we can listen for the break from that pattern of speech. This applies to individuals, and this applies to groups. The break from the pattern is where character lives, and where dialogue, ironically begins, in the *uh*, in the pause, in the thought as captured for the first time in a moment of speech, rather than in the rehearsed, the proven. Although this is a book, I must conclude by remarking that this project is at its heart, about the act of speech, the physical action of dialogue, and was not originally intended for the printed word. Our effort has been to try to document it in such a way that the act of speech is evident.

When I started On the Road, I asked a linguist for ways to listen for the breakdown of syntax. She gave me a set of questions to ask: 1) Have you ever come close to death?; 2) Have you ever been accused of something that you did not do?; 3) Do you remember the circumstances of your birth? I used the questions as a structure for all of my interviews. Indeed, those questions, and the answers taught me how to listen. I then discarded those questions. They served their purpose. When I was in Crown Heights, I interviewed Mr. Carmel Cato, the father of Gavin Cato. His interview is one of the most remarkable interviews I have collected. His language is completely distinct, poetic, and rich. When I was going back to Manhattan from Crown Heights on the subway, my head was racing with excitement about how he had spoken. I suddenly realized that he had answered all three of those questions. I hadn't asked them, and frankly I hadn't thought of those questions in a long time. Yes, he came close to death, the death of his son. Yes, he was accused of something he did not do, the police were beating him on the back while he was trying to lift the car off of his son. Yes, he remembered the circumstances of his birth, he gives an account of them. Mr. Cato's interview was a signal to me of something happening in America right now. In the year since Crown Heights, I have been interviewing people about the civil disturbance in Los Angeles in 1992 following the Rodney King verdict. Many people are answering one, if not all, of those questions. I don't ask those questions, but it comes up in many interviews. People have come close to death; they do feel accused of something that they didn't do, whether it's to be apprehended by the police for no other reason than being the wrong color in the wrong neighborhood, or because of the fear people have of being in any neighborhood at any time. Many people do remark on the circumstances of their "cultural" birth, their original nationality, their ethnicity. American character is alive inside of syntactical breaks.

During my search for character, I have learned much more than I set out to learn. I am still in the process of learning how the language of groups reflects the character of the group. Some of the same signals that apply with individuals may apply. In these times when we are re-thinking cultural identity I am interested in the difficulty people have in talking about race and talking about difference. This difficulty goes across race, class, and political lines. I am interested in the lack of words and mistrustful of the ease with which some people seem to pick up new words and mix them in with the old. The new words seem to get old quickly. This means to me that we do not have a language that serves us as a group. I think that there is a gap between those who are heard and those who speak. Those who really speak in their own communities, to their own people, are not heard as frequently as those who speak on a regular basis with authority. The media most often goes to experts to learn about difference. My sense is that American character lives not in one place or the other, but in the gaps between the places, and in our struggle to be together in our differences. It lives not in what has been fully articulated, but in what is in the process of being articulated, not in the smooth-sounding words, but in the very moment that the smooth-sounding words fail us. It is alive right now. We might not like what we see, but in order to change it, we have to see it clearly.

The Crown Heights Conflict: Background Information

On August 19, 1991, in the Crown Heights section of Brooklyn, New York, one of the cars in a three-car procession carrying the Lubavitcher Hasidic rebbe (spiritual leader) ran a red light, hit another car, and swerved onto the sidewalk. The car struck and killed Gavin Cato, a seven-year-old Black boy from Guyana, and seriously injured his cousin Angela.

As rumors spread that a Hasidic-run ambulance service helped the driver and his passengers while the children lay bleeding, members of the district's Black community reacted with violence against the police and the Lubavitchers. That evening, a group of young Black men fatally stabbed Yankel Rosenbaum, a 29-year-old Hasidic scholar from Australia. For three days, Black people fought police, attacked Lubavitcher headquarters, and torched businesses while Hasidic patrols responded with their own violence.

The conflict reflected long-standing tensions within Crown Heights between Lubavitchers and Blacks, as well as the pain, oppression, and discrimination these groups have historically experienced outside their own communities. Members of the Crown Heights Black community, many of them Caribbean immigrants without U.S. citizenship from Jamaica, Guyana, Trinidad and Tobago, Haiti, and other countries, face discrimination both on the basis of their color and their national origin. And the Lubavitchers—members of an Orthodox Jewish sect that fled the Nazi genocide of Jews in Europe during World War II—are particularly vulnerable to anti-Jewish stereotyping because of their religious style of dress and insular community.

Many Blacks and others have said that White racism plays a critical role in Crown Heights. Black leaders have charged that the Lubavitchers have enjoyed "preferential treatment" in the community from police and other city agencies, including permission to close off major city streets during Jewish holidays. Blacks also report that some Lubavitchers have threatened and harassed them when buying area buildings for the expanding Lubavitcher community. Hasidic crime patrols, Blacks say, have indiscriminately targeted members of the Black community.

According to Jews and others, Black anti-Semitism has also played a significant role in the conflict. In addition to reporting that they are the frequent victims of Black street crime, Lubavitchers point to the August fighting that included calls to "Kill the Jews," "Get the Jews out," and chants of "Heil Hitler." Other statements during the conflict by some Black spokespeople about Hasidic "diamond merchants" and Jews as the "devil leaders" of White people evoked old stereotypes of a sinister conspiracy by rich Jews controlling things behind the scenes.

Many young Blacks who took to the streets in August 1991 were less interested in targeting Jews than in fighting the police, whom many in New York City's Black commu-

nity regard as an occupying army. During the conflict, police beat up Black reporters and arrested between 150 and
300 young Blacks as a "preventive measure" in what wit-
nesses described as indiscriminate "sweeps." Many of
those arrested were held for days without any word to
their families.

Like the Black community, the Lubavitchers have also
felt victimized during the conflict by the legal system and
view the jury acquittal of Yankel Rosenbaum's accused
murderer as the most stark example of this mistreatment.

Media coverage of the Crown Heights conflict has in-
tensified misunderstanding and hatred. Black media re-
ports generally presented the conflict as an anti-racist
struggle and dismissed or trivialized charges of anti-Semitism. Jewish newspapers often blamed "black agitators"
and spoke of "pogroms" (organized massacres of Jews).
The mainstream media, criticized by both Blacks and
Lubavitchers, tended to focus on Whites as victims and
Blacks as victimizers. This kind of media polarization has
made it extremely difficult for people to develop an understanding of the Crown Heights situation that acknowledges
the experiences of all people involved.

Crown Heights, Brooklyn
A Chronology

8:20 P.M. A station wagon from a police-escorted entourage bearing Lubavitcher Grand Rebbe Menachem Schneerson careens into two Guyanese American children at the intersection of Utica Avenue and President Street. Seven-year-old Gavin Cato is killed, and his cousin Angela suffers a broken leg. As an angry crowd gathers, the twenty-two-year-old Hasidic driver, Yosef Lifsh, and his two Hasidic passengers are taken from the scene by a private Jewish ambulance.

11:30 P.M. Three hours later and five blocks from the car accident, Yankel Rosenbaum, a visiting twenty-nine-year-old Hasidic history professor from Melbourne, Australia, is stabbed. Just after the incident, sixteen-year-old Lemrick Nelson, Jr., a Trinidadian American from Brooklyn, is arrested in connection with the stabbing.

August 20

2:00 A.M. Yankel Rosenbaum dies at Kings County Hospital.

PRE-DAWN Rioting begins on the streets, as Blacks and Lubavitchers set fires, throw stones and bottles, and unleash insults at each other and at the police. The rioting continues throughout the day.

Yosef Lifsh leaves the United States for Israel.

By the end of the day, police report sixteen arrests and twenty policemen injured.

August 21

8:15 A.M. Yankel Rosenbaum's funeral held at Lubavitch World Headquarters in Crown Heights. Afterward, Rosenbaum's body is flown back to Australia for burial.

Rioting continues and several stores are looted.

Before leading a march of nearly two hundred Blacks down Eastern Parkway, the Reverend Al Sharpton and Alton Maddox hold a news conference demanding Yosef Lifsh's arrest.

New York mayor David Dinkins and New York police Commissioner Lee Brown visit Crown Heights to urge peace, but both are silenced by rocks and bottles and insults.

Lemrick Nelson, Jr., is charged with the second-degree murder of Yankel Rosenbaum.

August 22

Rioting continues.

Police presence in Crown Heights is increased to over fifteen hundred officers. By the end of the day, police report 107 arrests overall.

August 24

Led by the Reverend Al Sharpton and Alton Maddox, approximately fifteen hundred protesters march through Crown Heights, while nearly as many police officers patrol the immediate area.

August 26

Gavin Cato's funeral is held in Brooklyn. The Reverend Al Sharpton delivers the eulogy.

September 5

The Brooklyn grand jury does not indict Yosef Lifsh in the death of Gavin Cato.

September 17

The Reverend Al Sharpton flies to Israel to notify Yosef Lifsh of a civil suit brought against him by the Cato family. The day is the Jewish holiday of Yom Kippur.

January 26, 1992

The Cato apartment is destroyed by fire. Fire officials determine the fire resulted from children playing with matches.

April 5

Lubavitchers demonstrate outside City Hall to mourn Yankel Rosenbaum and demand more arrests in connection with his slaying.

April 13

Brooklyn district attorney Charles Hynes says that it is

unlikely there will be more arrests in connection with the death of Yankel Rosenbaum.

October 29

5:20 P.M. Lemrick Nelson, Jr., is acquitted of all four counts charged against him in the killing of Yankel Rosenbaum.

8:40 P.M. More than one thousand Hasidic Jews rally outside Lubavitch headquarters in Crown Heights. Some bottle throwing and shouting matches ensue. Police report one arrest.

Mayor Dinkins offers a $10,000 reward for information leading to the conviction of Yankel Rosenbaum's murderer.

October 30

New York governor Mario Cuomo orders a state review of the case.

New York police commissioner Raymond Kelly asks his chief of detectives, Joseph R. Borrelli, to review the entire case from the scene of the accident to the announcement of the verdict.

November 15

Despite Governor Cuomo's assertion that Mayor Dinkins

is being unfairly blamed for Rosenbaum's death and the
unrest in Crown Heights, the Hasidic community continues to harshly criticize the mayor for his handling of the
riots.

November 17

The Lubavitch community files a federal class-action lawsuit alleging that the Dinkins administration and police department refused to conduct "any meaningful investigation" into the rioting and failed to "seek out perpetrators
aggressively."

November 25

In a locally televised speech, Mayor Dinkins defends his role in the Crown Heights disturbances.

December 3

Mayor Dinkins is heckled and called a "Jew Hater" at a Democratic club meeting in Queens.

April 30, 1993

United States District Court Judge Reena Raggi refuses to dismiss a lawsuit filed by the Lubavitch community that charges that city and police officials discriminated against Jews during the 1991 riots.

July 21

New York State Director of Criminal Justice Richard Girgenti releases a six-hundred-page report on the Crown Heights disturbances. The report is critical of both Mayor Dinkins's and former Police Commissioner Lee Brown's management and leadership during the disturbances, as well as the police investigation into Yankel Rosenbaum's death and the judge's conduct of the ensuing trial of Lemrick Nelson, Jr. The report is sent to United States Attorney General Janet Reno, whose department is investigating possible civil rights violations.

The Characters

Ntozake Shange

Playwright, poet, novelist.

Anonymous Lubavitcher Woman

Preschool teacher.

George C. Wolfe

Playwright, director, producing director of the New York Shakespeare Festival.

Aaron M. Bernstein

Physicist at Massachusetts Institute of Technology.

Anonymous Girl

Junior high school black girl of Haitian descent. Lives in Brooklyn near Crown Heights.

The Reverend Al Sharpton

Well-known New York activist, minister.

Rivkah Siegal

Lubavitcher woman, graphic designer.

Angela Davis

Author, orator, activist, scholar. Professor in the History of Consciousness Department at the University of California, Santa Cruz.

Monique "Big Mo" Matthews

Los Angeles rapper.

Leonard Jeffries

Professor of African American Studies at City University of New York, former head of the department.

Letty Cottin Pogrebin

Author *Deborah, Golda, and Me*. One of the founding editors of *Ms.* magazine.

Minister Conrad Mohammed

New York minister for the Honorable Louis Farrakhan.

Robert Sherman

Director, Mayor of the City of New York's Increase the Peace Corps.

Rabbi Joseph Spielman

Spokesperson in the Lubavitch community.

The Reverend Canon Doctor Heron Sam

Pastor, St. Mark's, Crown Heights Church.

Anonymous Young Man #1

Crown Heights resident.

Michael S. Miller

Executive Director at the Jewish Community Relations Council.

Henry Rice

Crown Heights resident.

Norman Rosenbaum

Brother of Yankel Rosenbaum. A barrister from Australia.

Anonymous Young Man #2

African American young man, late teens, early twenties. Resident of Crown Heights.

Sonny Carson

Activist.

Rabbi Shea Hecht

Lubavitcher rabbi, spokesperson.

Richard Green

Director, Crown Heights Youth Collective. Codirector Project CURE, a Black-Hasidic basketball team that developed after the riots.

Roslyn Malamud

Lubavitcher resident of Crown Heights.

Reuven Ostrov

Lubavitcher youth, member, project CURE; at the time of the riot, was seventeen years old. Worked as assistant chaplain at Kings County Hospital.

Carmel Cato

Father of Gavin Cato. Crown Heights resident, originally from Guyana.

Production History

Fires in the Mirror had its world premiere at the New York Shakespeare Festival in New York City on May 1, 1992, with an official press opening on May 12.

The production closed in New York City on August 16, 1992, and, subsequently has been presented by the American Repertory Theatre in Cambridge, Massachusetts; the McCarter Theatre in Princeton, New Jersey; Brown University; Stanford University; the Brooklyn Academy of Music; and the Royal Court Theatre in London, among others.

The piece was conceived, written, and performed by Anna Deavere Smith and directed by Christopher Ashley.

All material is taken from interviews conducted by Anna Deavere Smith except: Angela Davis's "Rope," which is taken from an interview by Anna Deavere Smith and Thulani Davis; and Norman Rosenbaum's "My Brother's Blood," which is extracted from his speech at a rally, with the permission of Norman Rosenbaum and Beth Galinsky.

James Youmans designed the set; Candice Donnelly, the costumes; Debra J. Kletter, the lighting; Wendall K. Harrington and Emmanuelle Krebs, the projections; Brian Palmer, Linda Rosier, and Jim Tynan, the photographs; Joseph Jarman, the original musical score. Thulani Davis was the Dramaturg. Karen Moore was the Production Stage Manager.

Fires in the Mirror is part of a series of solo pieces created and performed by Ms. Smith called "On the Road: A Search for American Character," which includes pieces created for the Eureka Theatre, San Francisco, 1990 (*From the Outside Looking In*); the Rockefeller Conference Center, Bellagio, Italy (*Fragments: On the Intercultural Performance*); Crossroads Theatre (*Black Identity and Black Theatre*); Princeton University, New Jersey, (*Gender Bending*); and others.

The Crown Heights material in *Fires in the Mirror* was first created by George C. Wolfe's Festival of New Voices at the Joseph Papp Public Theatre in December 1991.

An adapted version of the play was filmed by "American Playhouse" under the direction of George C. Wolfe and starring Ms. Smith. It was produced by Cherie Fortis.

Fires in the Mirror

Ntozake Shange
The Desert

(This interview was done on the phone at about 4:00 P.M.
Philadelphia time. The only cue Ntozake gave about her
physical appearance was that she took one earring off to
talk on the phone. On stage we placed her upstage center
in an arm chair, smoking. Then we placed her standing,
downstage.)

Hummmm.

Identity—

it, is, uh…in a way it's, um…it's sort of, it's uh…

it's a psychic sense of place

it's a way of knowing I'm not a rock or that tree?

I'm this other living creature over here?

And it's a way of knowing that no matter where I put
    myself

that I am not necessarily

what's around me.

I am part of my surroundings

and I become separate from them

and it's being able to make those differentiations clearly

that lets us have an identity

and what's inside our identity

is everything that's ever happened to us.

Everything that's ever happened

to us as well as our responses to it

'cause we might be alone in a trance state,

someplace like the desert

and we begin to feel as though

we are part of the desert—
which we are right at that minute—
but we are not the desert,
uh...
we are part of the desert,
and when we go home
we take with us that part of the desert that the desert gave us,
but we're still not the desert.
It's an important differentiation to make because you
    don't know
what you're giving if you don't know what you have and
    you don't
know what you're taking if you don't know what's yours
    and what's
somebody else's.

Anonymous Lubavitcher Woman Static

(This interview was actually done on the phone. Based on what she told me she was doing, and on the three visits I had made to her home for other interviews, I devised this physical scene. A Lubavitcher woman, in a wig, and loose-fitting clothes. She is in her mid-thirties. She is folding clothes. There are several children around. Three boys of different ages are lying together on the couch. The oldest is reading to the younger two. A teen-age girl with long hair, a button-down-collar shirt, and skirt is sweeping the floor.)

Well,

it was um,

getting toward the end of Shabbas,

like around five in the afternoon,

and it was summertime

and sunset isn't until about eight, nine o'clock,

so there were still quite a few hours left to go

and my baby had been playing with the knobs on the
    stereo system

then all of a sudden he pushed the button—

the *on* button—

and all of a sudden came blaring out,

at full volume,

sort of like a half station

of polka music.

But just like with the static,

it was blaring, blaring

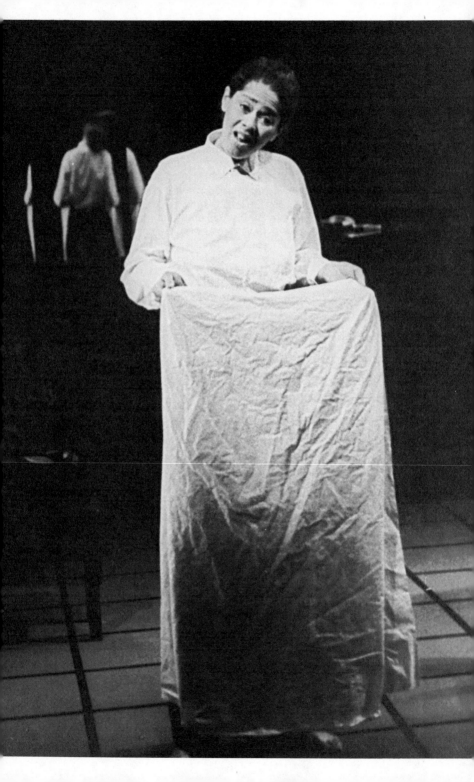

and we can't turn off,
we can't turn off electrical,
you know electricity, on Shabbas.
So um,
uh...
there was—
we just were trying to ignore it,
but a young boy that was visiting us,
he was going nuts already, he said
it was giving him such a headache could we do something
    about it,
couldn't we get a baby
to turn it off;
we can't make the baby turn it off but if the baby,
but if a child under three
turns something on or turns something off it's not
    considered against the Torah,
so we put the baby by it and tried to get the baby to turn it off,
he just probably made it worse,
so the guest was so uncomfortable that I said I would go
    outside
and see if I can find someone who's not Jewish and see if
    they would
like to—
see if they could turn it off,
so you can have somebody who's not Jewish do a simple
    act like
turning on the light or turning off the light,
and I hope I have the law correct,
but you can't ask them to do it directly.
If they wanna do it of their own free will—

and hopefully they would get some benefit from it too,
so I went outside
and I saw
a little
boy in the neighborhood
who I didn't know and didn't know me—
not Jewish, he was black and he wasn't wearing a
    yarmulke because you can't—
so I went up to him and I said to him
that my radio is on really loud and I can't turn it off,
could he help me,
so he looked at me a little crazy like,
Well?
And I said I don't know what to do,
so he said okay,
so he followed me into the house
and he hears this music on so loud
and so unpleasant
and so
he goes over to the
stereo
and he says, "You see this little button here
that says on and off?
Push that in
and that turns it off."
And I just sort of stood there looking kind of dumb
and then he went and pushed it,
and we laughed that he probably thought:
And people say Jewish people are really smart and they
    don't know
how to turn off their radios.

Anna Deavere Smith

George C. Wolfe
101 Dalmations

(The Mondrian Hotel in Los Angeles. Morning, Sunny. A very nice room. George is wearing denim jeans, a light blue denim shirt, and white leather tennis shoes. His hair is in a ponytail. He wears tortoise/wire spectacles. He is drinking tea with milk. The tea is served on a tray, the cups and teapot are delicate porcelain. George is sitting on a sofa, with his feet up on the coffee table.)

I mean I grew up on a black—
a one-block street—
that was black.
My grandmother lived on that street
my cousins lived around the corner.
I went to this
Black— Black—
private Black grade school
where
I was extraordinary.
Everybody there was extraordinary.
You were told you were extraordinary.
It was very clear
that I could not go to see *101 Dalmations* at the Capital
      Theatre
because it was segregated.
And at the same time
I was treated like I was the most extraordinary creature
      that had
been born.
So I'm on my street in my house,

at my school—
and I was very spoiled too—
so I was treated like I was this special special creature.
And then I would go beyond a certain point
I was treated like I was insignificant.
Nobody was
hosing me down or calling me nigger.
It was just that I was insignificant.
(Slight pause)
You know what I mean so it was very clear of
(Teacup on saucer strike twice on "very clear")
where my extraordinariness lived.
You know what I mean.
That I was extraordinary as long as I was Black.
But I am—not—going—to place myself
(Pause)
in relationship to your whiteness.
I will talk about your whiteness if we want to talk about that.
But I,
but what,
that which,
what I—
what am I saying?
My blackness does not resis— ex— re—
exist in relationship to your whiteness.
(Pause)
You know
(Not really a question, more like a hum)
(Slight pause)
it does not exist in relationship to—

Anna Deavere Smith

it *exists*
it exists.
I come—
you know what I mean—
like I said, I, I, I,
I come from—
it's a very com*plex*,
con*fused*,
neu-rotic,
at times destructive
reality, but it is completely
and totally a reality
contained and, and,
and full unto itself.
It's complex.
It's demonic.
It's ridiculous.
It's absurd.
It's evolved.
It's all the stuff.
That's the way I grew up.
(Slight pause)
So that *therefore*—
and then you're White—
(Quick beat)
And then there's a point when,
and then these two things come into contact.

Anna Deavere Smith

Aaron M. Bernstein
Mirrors and
Distortions

(Evening, Cambridge, Massachusetts. Fall. He is a man in
his fifties, wearing a sweater and a shirt with a pen guard.
He is seated at a round wooden table with a low-hanging
lamp.)

Okay, so a mirror is something that reflects light.
It's the simplest instrument to understand,
okay?
So a simple mirror is just a flat
reflecting
substance, like,
for example,
it's a piece of glass which is silvered on the back,
okay?
Now the notion of distortion also goes back into literature,
okay?
I'm trying to remember from art—
You probably know better than I.
You know you have a pretty young woman and she looks
     in a mirror
and she's a witch
(He laughs)
because she's evil on the inside.
That's not a real mirror,
as everyone knows—
where

you see the inner thing.
Now that really goes back in literature.
So everyone understood that mirrors don't distort,
so that was a play
not on words
but a concept.
But physicists do
talk about distortion.
It's a big
subject, distortions.
I'll give you an example—
if you wanna see the
stars
you make a big
reflecting mirror—
that's one of the ways—
you make a big telescope
so you can gather in a lot of light
and then it focuses at a point
and then there's always something called the circle of
     confusion.
So if ya don't make the thing perfectly spherical or
     perfectly
parabolic
then,
then, uh, if there are errors in the construction
which you can see, it's easy, if it's huge,
then you're gonna have a circle of confusion,
you see?
So that's the reason for making the

telescope as large as you can,
because you want that circle
to seem smaller,
and you want to easily see errors in the construction.
So, you see, in physics it's very practical—
if you wanna look up in the heavens
and see the stars as well as you can
without distortion.
If you're counting stars, for example,
and two look like one,
you've blown it.

Anonymous Girl
Look in the Mirror

(Morning. Spring. A teen-age Black girl of Haitian descent. She has hair which is straightened, and is wearing a navy blue jumper and a white shirt. She is seated in a stairwell at her junior high school in Brooklyn.)

When I look in the mirror . . .
I don't know.
How did I find out I was Black . . .
(Tongue sound)
When I grew up and I look in the mirror and saw I was
    Black.
When I look at my parents,
That's how I knew I was Black.
Look at my skin.
You Black?
Black is beautiful.
I don't know.
That's what I always say.
I think White is beautiful too.
But I think Black is beautiful too.
In my class nobody is White, everybody's Black,
and some of them is Hispanic.
In my class
you can't call any of them Puerto Ricans.
They despise Puerto Ricans, I don't know why.
They think that Puerto Ricans are stuck up and
    everything.

Anna Deavere Smith

They say, Oh my Gosh my nail broke, look at that cute
    guy and everything.
But they act like that themselves.
They act just like White girls.
Black girls is not like that.
Please, you should be in my class.
Like they say that Puerto Ricans act like that
and they don't see that they act like that themselves.
Black girls, they do bite off the Spanish girls,
they bite off of your clothes.
You don't know what that means? biting off?
Like biting off somebody's clothes
Like cop, following,
and last year they used to have a lot of girls like that.
They come to school with a style, right?
And if they see another girl with that style?
Oh my gosh look at her.
What she think she is,
she tryin' to bite off of me in some way
no don't be bitin' off of my sneakers
or like that.
Or doin' a hairstyle
I mean Black people are into hairstyles.
So they come to school, see somebody with a certain style,
they say uh-huh I'm gonna get me one just like that uh-huh,
that's the way Black people are
Yea-ah!
They don't like people doing that to them
and they do that to other people,
so the Black girls will follow the Spanish girls.

The Spanish girls don't bite off of us.
Some of the Black girls follow them.
But they don't mind
They don't care.
They follow each other.
Like there's three girls in my class,
they from the Dominican Republic.
They all stick together like glue.
They all three best friends.
They don't follow nobody,
like there's none of them lead or anything.
They don't hang around us either.
They're
by themselves.

Anna Deavere Smith

The Reverend Al Sharpton Me and James's Thing

(Early afternoon. Fall. A small room that is a part of a suite of offices in a building on West Fifty-seventh Street and Seventh Avenue in New York. A very large man Black man with straightened hair. Reverend Sharpton's hair is in the style of James Brown's hair. He is wearing a suit, colorful tie, and a gold medallion that was given to him by Martin Luther King, Jr. Reverend Sharpton has a pinky ring, a very resonant voice even in this small room. There is a very built, very tall man who sits behind me during the interview. Reverend Sharpton's face is much younger, and more innocent than it appears to be in the media. His humor is in his face. He is very direct. The interview only lasts fifteen minutes because he had been called out of a meeting in progress to do the interview.)

James Brown raised me.
Uh...
I never had a father.
My father left when I was ten.
James Brown took me to the beauty parlor one day
and made my hair like his.
And made me promise
to wear it like that
'til I die.
It's a personal family thing
between me and James Brown.
I always wanted a father
and he filled that void.
And the strength that he's demonstrated—

I don't know anybody that reached his heights,
and then had to go as low as he did and come back.
And I think that if anybody I met in life deserved that type of tribute from
somebody
that he wanted a kid
to look like him
and be like his son...
I just came home from spending a weekend with him now,
uh, uh,
I think James deserved that.
And just like
he was the father I never had,
his kids never even visited him when he went to jail.
So I was like the kid he never had.
And if I had to choose between arguing with people about my hairstyle
or giving him that one tribute
he axed,
I'd rather give him that tribute
because he filled a void for me.
And I really don't give a damn
who doesn't understand it.
Oh, I know not you, not you.
The press and everybody do
their thing on that.
It's a personal thing between me and James Brown.
And just like
in other communities
people do their cultural thing

with who they wanna look like,
uh,
there's nothing wrong with me doing
that with James.
It's, it's, *us*.
I mean in the fifties it was a slick.
It was acting like White folks.
But today
people don't wear their hair like that.
James and I the only ones out there doing that.
So it's certainlih not
a reaction to Whites.
It's me and James's thing.

Anna Deavere Smith

Rivkah Siegal
Wigs

Your hair—
It only has to be—
there's different,
u h m,
customs in different
Hasidic groups.
Lubavitch
the system is
it should be two inches
long.
It's—
some groups
have
the custom
to shave their
heads.
There's—
the reason is,
when you go to the mikvah [bath]
you may, maybe,

it's better if it's short
because of what you—
the preparation
that's involved
and that
you have to go under the water.
The hair has a tendency to float
and you have to be completely submerged
including your hair.
So...
And I got married
when I was a little older,
and I really wanted to be married
and I really wanted to, um . . .
In some ways I was eager to cover my head.
Now if I had grown up in a Lubavitch household

and then had to cut it,
I don't know what that would be like.
I really don't.
But now that I'm wearing the wig,
you see,
with my hair I can keep it very simple
and I can change it all the time.
So with a wig you have to have like five wigs if you want to
    do that.
But I, uh,
I feel somehow like it's fake,
I feel like it's not me.
I try to be as much myself as I can,
and it just
bothers me
that I'm kind of fooling the world.
I used to go to work.
People . . .
and I would wear a different wig,
and they'd say I like your new haircut
and I'd say it's not mine!
You know,
and it was very hard for me to say it
and
it became very difficult.
I mean, I've gone through a lot with wearing wigs and not
    wearing
wigs.
It's been a big issue for me.

Angela Davis
Rope

(Morning. Spring. Oakland, California. In reality this interview was done on the phone, with myself and Thulani
Davis. Thulani and I were calling from an office at the Public Theatre. We do not know exactly what Angela was doing
or wearing. I believe, from things she said, that she was
sitting on her deck in her home, which overlooks a beautiful panorama of trees.)

Race, um—
of course
for many years in the history
of African Americans in this country—
was synonymous with community.
As a matter of fact
we were race women and race men.
Billie Holiday for example
called herself a race woman
because she supported the community
and as a child growing up in the South
my assumptions were
that if anybody in the race
came under attack
then I had to be there
to support that person,
to support the race.
I was saying to my students just the other day,
I said,
if in 1970,
when I was

in jail,
someone had told me
that in 1991,
a Black man
who
said that his, um . . .
hero—
(Increased volume, speed, and energy)
one of his heroes
was Malcolm X—
would be nominated to the Supreme Court
I would have celebrated
and I don't think it would have been possible at that time
to convince me
that I would
be absolutely opposed,
a Black candidate—
I mean like absolutely—
(A new attack, more energy)
or that if anyone would have told me that
a *woman* . . .
finally be elected to the Supreme Court,
it would have been very difficult,
as critical as I am with respect to feminism,
as critical as I have always been with what I used to call,
you know, narrow nationalism?
I don't think
it would have been possible to convince me that things
    would have so absolutely
shifted that

someone could have evoked
the specter of lynching
on national television
and that specter of lynching would be used to violate our
    history.
And I still feel that
we have to point out the racism involved
in the razing of a Black man
and a Black woman
in that way.
I mean [Ted] Kennedy was sitting right there
and it had never occurred to anyone to bring him up
before
the world,
which is not to say that I don't think it should happen.
And it is actually a sign of how we,
in our various oppressed
marginalized communities,
have been able to turn
terrible acts of racism directed against us
into victory . . .
And therefore I think
Anita Hill did that,
and so it's very complicated,
but I have no problems aligning myself politically
against Clarence Thomas in a real passionate way,
but at the same time I can talk about the racism that led
to the possibility
of constructing those kinds of hearings
and

the same thing with Mike Tyson.
So I guess that would be,
um . . .
the way in which I would begin to look at community,
and would therefore think
that race has become, uh,
an increasingly obsolete way
of constructing community
because it is based on unchangeable
immutable biological
facts
in a very pseudo-scientific way,
alright?
Now
racism is entirely different
because see *racism*,
uh,
actually I think
is
at the origins of this concept of race.
It's not—
it's not the other way around,
that there were racists,
and then the racists—
one race came to dominate
the others.
As a matter of fact
in order for a European colonialist
to attempt
to conquer the world,

Anna Deavere Smith

to colonize the world,
they had to construct this notion
of,
uh,
the populations of the earth being divided into certain,
uh,
firm biological, uh,
communities,
and that's what I think we have to go back and look at.
So when I use the word race now I put it in quotations.
Because if we don't transform
this . . . this intransigent
rigid
notion of race,
we will be caught up in this cycle
of genocidal
violence
that, um,
is at the origins of our history.
So I think—
and I'm
I'm convinced—
and this is what I'm working on in my political practice
     right now—
is that we have to find ways of coming together in a
     different way,
not the old notion of coalition in which we anchor
     ourselves very solidly
in our,
um,

Fires in the Mirror   **31**

communities,

and simply voice

our

solidarity with other people.

I'm not suggesting that we do not anchor ourselves in our
    communities;

I feel very anchored in,

um,

my various communities,

but I think that,

you know,

to use a metaphor, the rope

attached to that anchor should be long enough to allow us
    to move

into other communities

to understand and learn.

I've been thinking a lot about the need to make more
    intimate

these connections and associations and to really take on
    the responsibility

of learning.

So I think that we need to—

in order to find ways of working with

and understanding

the vastness

of our many cultural heritages

and ways of coming together without

rendering invisible all of that heterogeneity—

I don't have the answer,

you know

Anna Deavere Smith

I don't know.
What I'm interested in is communities
that are not static,
that
can change, that can respond to new historical needs.
So I think it's a very exciting moment.

Monique "Big Mo" Matthews
Rhythm and Poetry

(In reality this interview was done on an afternoon in the spring of 1989, while I was in residence at the University of California, Los Angeles, as a fellow at the Center for Afro-American Studies. Mo was a student of mine. We were sitting in my office, which was a narrow office, with sunlight. I performed Mo in many shows, and in the course of performing her, I changed the setting to a performance setting, with microphone. I was inspired by a performance that I saw of Queen Latifah in San Francisco, and by Mo's behavior in my class, which was performance behavior, to change the setting to one that was more theatrical, since Mo's everyday speech was as theatrical as Latifah's performance speech. Speaking directly to the audience, pacing the stage.)

And she say, "This is for the fellas,"
and she took off all her clothes and she had on a leotard
that had all cuts and stuff in it,
and she started doin' it on the floor.
They were like
"Go, girl!"
People like, "That look really stink."
But that's what a lot of female rappers do—
like to try to get off,
they sell they body or pimp they body
to, um, get play.
And you have people like Latifah who doesn't, you know,
she talks intelligent.
You have Lyte who's just hard and people are scared by her
hardness,

her strength of her words.

She encompasses that whole, New York–street sound.

It's like, you know, she'll like…

what's a line?

What's a line

like "Paper Thin,"

"IN ONE EAR AND RIGHT OUT THE OTHUH."

It's like,

"I don't care what you have to say,

I'm gittin' done what's gotta be done.

Man can't come across me.

A female she can't stand against me.

I'm just the toughest, I'm just the hardest/You just can't
    come up

against me/if you do you get waxed!"

It's like a lot of my songs,

I don't know if I'm gonna get blacklisted for it.

The image that I want is a strong strong African strong
    Black woman

and I'm not down with what's going on, like Big Daddy
    Kane had a song

out called "Pimpin Ain't Easy," and he sat there and he
    talk for the

whole song, and I sit there I wanna slap him, I wanna slap
    him so

hard, and he talks about, it's one point he goes, yeah

u m,

"Puerto Rican girls Puerto Rican girls call me Papi and

White girls say

even White girls say I'm a hunk!"

I'm like,

"What you mean 'even'?

Oh! Black girls ain't good enough for you huh?"

And one of my songs has a line that's like

"PIMPIN' AIN'T EASY BUT WHORIN' AIN'T
    PROPER. RESPECT AND
CHERISH THE ORIGINAL MOTHER."

And a couple of my friends were like,

"Aww, Mo, you good but I can't listen to you 'cause you be Men
bashin'."

I say,

"It ain't men bashin', it's female assertin'."

Shit.

I'm tired of it.

I'm tired of my friends just acceptin'

that they just considered to be a ho.

You got a song,

"Everybody's a Hotty."

A "hotty" means you a freak, you a ho,

and it's like Too Short

gets up there and he goes,

"B I AYYYYYYYYYYYYE."

Like he stretches "bitch" out for as long as possible,

like you just a ho and you can't be saved,

and 2 Live Crew. . . . "we want some pussy," and the
    girls! "La le la le la le la,"

it's like my friends say,

"Mo, if you so bad how come you don't never say nothin
    about Two

Live Crew?"

When I talk about rap,
and I talk about people demeaning rap,
I don't even mention them
because they don't understand the fundamentals of rap.
Rap, rap
is basically
broken down
Rhythm
and Poetry.
And poetry is expression.
It's just like poetry; you release so much through poetry
    you get
angry, you get it?
Poetry is like
intelligence.
You just release it all and if you don't have a complex
    rhyme
it's like,
"I'm goin to the store."
What rhymes with store?
More store for more bore
"I'm going to the store I hope I don't get bored,"
it's like,
"WHAT YOU SAYIN', MAN? WHO CARES?"
You have to have something that flows.
You have to be def,
D-E-F.
I guess I have to think of something for you that ain't slang.
Def is dope, def is live
when you say somethin's dope

          Anna Deavere Smith

it means it is the epitome of the experience
and you have to be def by your very presence
because you have to make people happy.
And we are living in a society where people are not happy
    with their everyday lives.

Leonard Jeffries
Roots

(3:00 P.M. Wednesday, November 20, 1991. A very large conference room in the African American Studies Department at CUNY. Drawn venetian blinds, fluorescent lighting. Dr. Jeffries wears a light, multicolored African top, and a multicolored African hat. His shoes are black functional shoes, like the shoes to a uniform. He sits facing the table, and often sits back with the chair back from the table, often touches the table, and often sits back with the chair on its back legs only. Sometimes he scratches his head by throwing his hat forward on his head with great ease and authority. There is a bodyguard, a large heavyset African American man, present.)

People are asking who is this guy Jeffries?
When they find out my background they're gonna be
     surprised.
They are gonna find out that I was even related to Alex Haley.
In fact I was a major consultant for *Roots*.
In fact there might not have been a *Roots* without me.
Now when I say that,
that's my own personal in-group joke wit' Alex.
He was in Philadelphia
getting his ticket to go down to Jamaica
and
Roots was lost.
He had it in a duffle bag,
a big duffle bag like this,
the whole manuscript.
It was lost in the airport of Philadelphia.
I got on my horse and ran around the airport of
     Philadelphia

and found *Roots*.

So that's my joke.

He had this manuscript,

Alex didn't have anything else but this manuscript.

Now if he had lost that, that would have been it.

He didn't have any photocopies.

Alex did everything on a shoestring.

u h m

so for him to deny me now . . .

He never even acknowledged

Pat

Alexander

his girlfriend/secretary who he had paid with affection and
    not with

resources.

So I didn't expect him to acknowledge me.

He called me to come down.

I called my wife who was working on her Ph.D. at Yale.

I said, "Rosalind, Alex wants us to come down to
    Brunswick, Georgia,

they're filming *Roots*."

She said yes she'd come down and we'd go, then she called
    me back.

She said, "I got too much work," so I went down to
    Brunswick, Georgia.

He introduced me to Margulies,

who was the, um, director

of *Roots*,

as the leading expert in America on Africa, and I said,
    "Wow," to

myself, "that's kind of high."

When Margulies said,

"That makes me number two," then I realized what Alex
    was doing to keep *Roots* honest.

So for two weeks I tried to change *Roots*.

Alex would say, "Wait a

minute, let's consult the experts."

After two weeks they got tired of me, sat me down

and said, "Dr. Jeffries," at lunch,

"we are very happy to have you here

but we just bought the rights to the book *Roots*

and we are under no obligation to maintain the integrity of
    the book

and we certainly don't have to deal with the truth of Black
    history."

Now,

this was a wipeout for me

I

I, there's been very few trau*matic*

moments

(Longest pause in his text)

uh, just to think.

Now I wasn't even prepared for this

but Pat had called me before and said,

"Len, I'm looking at this document and I don't know what
    to make of it."

I said, "What is it, Pat, what is it?"

and I knew she was nervous, she said,

"I'm reading a contract that says

"*Roots* has been sold to David Wolper and their heirs for
    ever and

Anna Deavere Smith

ever

(He is thumping his hand on table)

and their heirs for ever and ever."

Alex had signed the contract for fifty thousand dollars.

(He is thumping his hand on table)

Fifty thousand dollars for paperback *Roots*.

Something that made how much?

Three hundred million dollars?

He was suing them for years.

The millions he made on TV *Roots* he spent a lot of it to
      sue

Doubleday to get a better deal—I don't know if he ever got
      it.

Roots was a devastation.

The tens of millions and hundreds of millions made on
      Roots

went to produce,

not to make more Black series,

like *Roots*,

but they went to produce a *series*

maybe a dozen mini-series on *Jewish* history

as opposed to Black history.

You can document what was produced in terms of Black
      history

compared to what was produced of Jewish history.

It's a devastation.

But the *one* thing that came out of this for me,

was that when these people told me, you know,

"We bought your research

We bought your history

You really have no . . ."

I was thrown off

I had to get out of there.

I stayed for another couple of days.

I told Alex I had to make a pilgrimage to my grandfather's
grave.

Never saw my grandfather.

Then I watched one more scene in the Alex Haley thing

and that finished it for me.

A cutaway of a slave ship

that was so real that they had to bring in these high school
kids,

and once these high school kids played the enslaved
Africans greased

down in simulated vomit

and feces

they couldn't come back,

so they had to continue to get,

go take these youngsters,

and some little White woman

who was there sleeping with one of those guys,

they told her, "You cannot take these kids without
authorization."

But she would drive a bus

up to the schoolyard,

put the kids in it, and bring them to the set.

And it almost produced a riot

there.

But anyway this slave scene

was so realistic

the trainer's up on a lower deck

Anna Deavere Smith

and Kunta Kinte's on a bottom deck
and they call down to each other,
and the trainer says,
"Kunta Kinte,
Be strong! Be strong!
We may have to fight.
Kill the White man and return to Mother Africa."
This was high drama.
All of us grown men over hiding in the shadows in *tears*.
Then
Green rushes out and said, "Break! Break!"
He said he didn't want the scene.
We said, "What?"
Even Lou Gossett and them were ready to *fight*!
You know 'cause they had—
a movie script is just
a skeleton,
you have to put your soul in a movie script,
and they put their heart and soul into what would have
    been . . .
And with the African—
because the "earth is mother" all over Africa.
So to say to go back to Mother Africa is a very meaningful
    phrase.
But this
Englishman refused
to accept it,
and they almost had a physical fight on the set.
They compromised and said,
"We—are—all—from—one—village,"

(Hitting his hand rhythmically on the desk)
which is not the same thing.
After that I said, "I have to go."
I said I have to go,
and I rented a—
I flew out with Lorne Greene of all people.
He saw me and we had known each other for a couple of
	weeks from
the set,
and he's sitting there drinking his little drinks
talking about "Isn't *Roots* wonderful.
It's everybody's history,"
and I'm dying.
(Pause)
Get to Atlanta.
Rent a car. Cut across the Georgia countryside.
came to a fork in the road,
made the right turn,
and there
on a bluff
was a clapboard church
made by my grandfather
and
four
other trustees.
Then when
I went across the cemetery
to see, uh,
the gravesite where he was—
the tallest tombstone in the graveyard was his.

Anna Deavere Smith

Uhm,

It was an obelisk.

On it was a Masonic symbol.

He was the master of the lodge.

On it was his vital statistics:

"Born August the tenth 1868."

At the birth of the Fourteenth Amendment.

I later learned that his brother Sam was born

1865 at the birth of the Thirteenth Amendment!

And this is why people say,

"Who is he?

What is he?

Why is he?"

If they only know

I've had one of the best educations on the planet.

Yeah.

So . . .

When I went to Albany

in July,

I went knowing that you might not have

much time,

just like my wife said on the radio today:

"When we speak

we speak as though it is the last speech we're gonna make."

But I knew what was at stake

ever since they branded me a conspiracy theorist,

February 12, 1990,

two-column editorial in the *New York Times*.

That was,

in the concept of Jewish thinking,

the kiss of death.
I knew I had been targeted.
Arthur Schlesinger went and wrote a book
called *The Disuniting of America*.
He has everybody in the margin
except a half-page photo of myself
which said to us,
"This is the one they got to kill."
We knew that Schlesinger
and his people had sent out a thousand letters
to CEOs around the country
and foundation heads
not to have anything to do with
all of us involved in these studies
for multicultural curriculum
so, uh . . .
Knowing that I had taken this beating for two and a half
    years
it was my chance to strike out,
but people don't understand
that that was my way of saying,
"You bastids! . . .
for starting this process
of destroying *me*."
That was my striking out.
But people don't know the context.
They don't know that for two and a half years
I bore this burden
by myself
and I bore it well.

         Anna Deavere Smith

And now they've got a problem.
'Cause after they destroyed me,
here he is resurrected!!!!!
I spoke at Columbia, I spoke at Queens College. . . .

Letty Cottin Pogrebin Near Enough to Reach

(Evening. The day before Thanksgiving, 1991. On the phone. Direct, passionate, confident, lots of volume. She is in a study with a rolltop desk and a lot of books.)

I think it's about rank frustration and the old story

that you pick a scapegoat

that's much more, I mean Jews and Blacks,

that's manageable,

because we're near,

we're still near enough to each other to reach!

I mean, what can you do about the people who voted for
        David Duke?

Are Blacks going to go there and deal with that?

No, it's much easier to deal with Jews who are also panicky.

We're the only ones that pay any attention

(Her voice makes an upward inflection)

Do you hear?

Well, Jeffries did speak about the Mafia being, um,

Mafia,

and the Jews in Hollywood.

I didn't see

this tremendous outpouring of Italian

reaction.

Only *Jews* listen,

only *Jews* take Blacks seriously,

only *Jews* view Blacks as full human beings that you

Anna Deavere Smith

should *address*
in their rage
and, um,
people don't seem to notice that.
But Blacks, it's like a little child kicking up against Arnold
Schwarzenegger
when they,
when they have anything to say about the dominant culture
nobody listens! Nobody reacts!
To get a headline,
to get on the evening news,
you have to attack a Jew.
Otherwise you're ignored.
And it's a shame.
We all play into it.

Minister Conrad Mohammed Seven Verses

(April 1992, morning. A café/restaurant. Roosevelt Island, New York. We are sitting in the back, in an area that is surrounded by glass floor-to-ceiling windows. Mr. Mohammed is impeccably dressed in a suit of an elegant fabric. He wears a blue shirt and a bow tie. He has on fine shoes, designer socks, and a large fancy watch and wedding ring. His hair is closely cropped. He drinks black coffee, and uses a few packs of sugar. He is traveling with another man, also a Muslim, in the clothing of a Muslim, impeccable, who sits at another table and watches us.)

The condition of the Black man in America today is part
    and parcel,
through the devlishment
that permitted Caucasian people
to rob us of our humanity,
and put us in the throes of slavery . . .
The fact that our— our Black
parents
were actually taken
as cattle
and as, as
animals
and packed into
slave ships
like sardines
amid feces
and urine—

and the suffering of our people,
for months,
in the middle passage—
Our women,
raped
before our own eyes,
so that today
some look like you,
some look like me,
some look like brother . . .
(Indicating his companion)
This is a crime of tremendous proportion.
In fact,
no crime in the history of humanity
has before or since
equaled that crime.
The Holocaust did not equal it
Oh, absolutely not.
First of all,
that was a horrible crime
and that is something that is a disgrace in the eyes of civilized
people.
That, uh, crime also stinks
in the nostrils of God.
But it in no way compares with the slavery of our people
because we lost over a hundred
and some say two hundred and fifty,
million
in the middle passage
coming from Africa

to America.
We were so thoroughly robbed.
We didn't just lose six million.
We didn't just
endure this
for, for
five or six years
or from '38 to '45 or '39 to —
We endured this for over three hundred years—
the total subjugation of the Black man.
You can go into Bangladesh today,
Calcutta,
(He strikes the table with a sugar packet three or four times)
New Delhi,
Nigeria,
some really
so-called underdeveloped nation,
and I don't care how low that person's humanity is
(He opens the sugar packet)
whether they never
had running water,
if they'd never seen a television or anything.
They are in better condition than the Black man and woman
in America today
right now.
Even at Harvard.
They have a contextual understanding of what identity is.
(He strikes the table with another sugar packet three or four times and opens it)

But the Black man has no knowledge of that;
he's an amnesia victim
(Starts stirring his coffee)
He has lost knowledge of himself
(Stirring his coffee)
and he's living a beast life.
(Stirring his coffee)
So this proves that it was the greatest
crime.
Because we were cut off from our past.
Not only were we killed and murdered,
not only were our women raped
in front of their own children.
Not only did the slave master stick
(The spoon drops onto saucer)
at times,
daggers into a pregnant woman's stomach,
slice the stomach open
push the baby out on the ground and crush the head of the
    baby
to instill fear in the Massas of the plantation.
(Stirring again)
Not only were these things done,
not only were our thumbs
(Spoon drops)
put in, in devices
that would just
slowly torture the slave
and tear the thumb off from the root.
Not only were we sold on the auction block

like cattle,
not permitted to marry.
See these are the crimes
of slavery that nobody wants to talk about.
But the most significant crime—
because we could have recovered from all of that—
but the fact that they cut off all knowledge from us,
told us that we were animals,
told us that we were subhuman,
took from us our names,
gave us names like
Smith
and Jones
and today we wear those names
with dignity
and pride,
yet these were the names given to us in one of the greatest
    crimes
ever committed on the face of the earth.
So this kind of thing,
Sister,
is what qualifies slavery
as the greatest
crime
ever committed.
They have stolen
our garment.
Stolen our identity.
The Honorable Louis Farrakhan
teaches us

that *we* are the chosen of God.
We are those people
that almighty God Allah
has selected as his chosen,
and they are masquerading in our garment—
the Jews.
We don't have an identity today.
Because we are the people . . .
There are seven verses
in the Bible,
seven verses,
I believe it is in Deuteronomy,
that the Jews base
their chosen people, uh, uh,
claim the theology,
the whole theological exegesis
with respect
of being the chosen
is based upon seven verses
in the Scripture that talk
about a covenant
with Abraham.

Anna Deavere Smith

Letty Cottin Pogrebin
Isaac

(Morning. Spring. On the phone. She is in her office in her home on West 67th Street and Central Park West in Manhattan. Her office has an old-fashioned wooden rolltop desk and bookcases filled with books. She says she was wearing leggings and a loose shirt.)

Well,
it's hard for me to do that
because
I think there's a tendency to make hay
with the Holocaust,
to push
all the buttons.
And I mean this story about my uncle Isaac—makes *me* cry
and it's going to make your audience cry
and I'm beginning to worry
that
we're trotting out our Holocaust stories
too regularly and that we're going to inure each other to
    the truth of
them.
But
I think
maybe if you let me read it,
I would prefer to read it:
(*Reading from* Deborah, Golda, and Me)
"I remember my mother's cousin

Isaac who came to New York
immediately after the war and lived with us for several
    months.
Isaac is my connection to dozens of other family members who
were murdered in the concentration camps.
Because he was blond and blue-eyed he had been
chosen as the designated survivor of his town.
That is the Jewish councils had instructed him to do
    anything
to stay alive and tell the story.
For Isaac
anything turned out to mean this.
The Germans suspected his forged Aryan papers and
    decided that he
would have to prove by his actions that he was not a Jew.
They put him on a transport train with the Jews of his town
and then gave him the task of herding into the gas chambers
everyone in his train load.
After he had fulfilled that assignment
with patriotic
German efficiency,
the Nazis accepted the authenticity of his identity papers
and let him go.
Among those whom Isaac packed into the gas chambers
    that day
dispassionately as if shoving a few more items into an
    overstuffed
closet
were his wife
and

two children.
The designated survivor
arrived in America
at about age forty
(Breathes in)
with prematurely white hair and a dead gaze within the
    sky blue
eyes that'd helped save his life.
As promised he told his story to dozens of Jewish agencies
and community leaders and to groups of families and
    friends which
is how I heard the account
translated from his Yiddish
by my mother.
For months he talked,
speaking the unspeakable.
Describing a horror
that American Jews had suspected but could not conceive.
A monstrous tale
that dwarfed the demonology of legend
and gave me the nightmare I still dream to this day.
And as he talked
Isaac seemed to grow older and older
until one night
a few months later
when he finished telling everything he knew
he died."

Robert Sherman
Lousy Language

(11:00 A.M. Wednesday, November 13, 1991. A very sunny and large, elegant living room in a large apartment near the Brooklyn Museum. Mr. Sherman is sitting in an armchair near an enormous bouquet of flowers for the birth of his first child. He wears sweats, and a bright orange long-sleeved tee shirt. Smiles frequently, upbeat, impassioned. Fingers his wedding ring. Each phrase builds on the next, pauses are all sustained intensity, never lets up. Full. Lots of volume, clear enunciation, teeth, and tongue very involved in his speech. Good-humored, seems to like the act of speech.)

Do you have demographic information on Crown Heights?

The important thing to remember is that—

and I will check these numbers when I get back to the
     office—

I think the

Hasidim

comprise only ten percent

of the population

of the neighborhood.

The Crown Heights conflict has been brewing on and off
     for twenty years

since the Hasidic community

developed some serious numbers

and some strength in Crown Heights and as African
     Americans and

Caribbean Americans came to make up the dominant
     culture in

Crown Heights.

Very important to remember that
those things that are expressed really as
bias,
those things
that we at the Human Rights Commission
would consider to be bias,
have the same trappings of bias,
which is complaints based on a characteristic, not on
    a knowledge of a
specific person.
There sort of is a soup
of bias—
prejudice, racism, and discrimination.
I think bias really does relate to
feelings with a valence,
feelings with a, uhm,
(Breathing in)

feelings that can go in a direction positive or negative
although we usually use bias to mean a negative.
What it means usually
is negative attitudes
that can lead to negative behaviors:
biased
acts, biased incidents,
or biased crimes.
Racism is hatred based on race.
Discrimination refers to
acts against somebody . . .
so that the words
actually tangle up.
I think in part
because vocabulary
follows general awareness. . . .
I think you know
the Eskimos have seventy words for snow?
We probably have seventy different kinds of bias,
        prejudice, racism, and

discrimination,
but it's not in our mind-set to be clear about it,
so I think that we have
sort of lousy language
on the subject
and that
is a reflection
of our unwillingness
to deal with it honestly
and to sort it out.
I think we have very, very bad language.

Anna Deavere Smith

Rabbi Joseph Spielman No Blood in His Feet

(9:30 A.M. Tuesday, November 12, 1991. A large home on President Street in Crown Heights. Only natural light, not very much light. Dark wood. A darkish dining room with an enormous table, could seat twenty. The rabbi sits at the head of the table. Lots of stuff on the table. He wears Hasidic clothing, a black fedora, black jacket, and reading glasses. As he talks, he slightly slides around the tape-recorder microphone, which is in front of him at the table. The furniture in the dining room including his chair is, for the most part, very old, solid wood. There are children playing quietly in another room, and people come in and out frequently, but always whispering and walking carefully not to make noise, unless they speak to him directly. The children at one point came over and stared at me.)

Many people were on the sidewalk,

talking, playing,

drinking

beer or whatever—

being that type of neighborhood.

A car

driven by an individual—

a Hasidic individual—

went through the intersection,

was hit by another car,

thereby causing it to go onto the sidewalk.

The driver on seeing

himself in such a position that he felt he was going to
    definitely hit

someone,

because of the amount of people on the sidewalk,

he steered at the building,

so as to get out of the way of the people.

Obviously, for the most part,

he was successful.

But regrettably,

one child was killed

and another child

was wounded.

Um,

seeing what happened,

he jumped out of the car

and, realizing

there may be a child under the car,

he tried to physically lift

the car

from the child.

Well, as he was doing this

the Afro-Americans were beating him already.

He was beaten so much he needed stitches in the scalp and
the face,

fifteen or sixteen stitches

and also

there were three other passengers in the car

that were being beaten too.

One of the passengers was calling 911

on the cellular phone.

A Black person

pulled the phone out of his hand and ran.

Anna Deavere Smith

Just stole the—stole the telephone.
The Jewish community
has a volunteer
ambulance corps
which is funded totally from the nations—
there is not one penny of government funds—
and manned by volunteers—
who many times at their expense—
supplied the equipment that they carry in order to save
    lives.
As one of the EMS ambulances were coming,
one of the Hasidic ambulances or the Jewish ambulances
    came
on the scene.
The EMS responded with three ambulances on the scene.
They were there before
the Jewish ambulance came.
Two or three police cars were already on the scene.
The police saw the potential for violence
and saw that the occupants of the car
were being beaten and were afraid for their safety.
At the same time the EMS asked

the Hasidic ambulances for certain pieces of equipment
     that they
were out of,
that they needed to take care of the Cato kid,
and,
um,
in fact, I was . . .
The Hasidic ambulance left, leaving behind one of the
     passengers.
That passenger had a walkie-talkie and he requested that I
come down to pick him up.
And at that time there was a lot of screaming and shouting
and it was a mixed crowd, Hasidic and Afro-American.
The police said, "Rabbi get your people out of here."
I told them to leave and I left.
Now,
a few hours later,
two and a half hours later,
in a different part of Crown Heights,
a scholar
from Australia,
Yankel Rosenbaum,
who, urr,
I think he had a doctorate or he was working on his
     doctorate,
was walking on the street
on his own—
I mean he was totally oblivious—
and he was accosted by a group of young Blacks
about twenty of them strong

which was being egged on by a Black
male approximately
forty years old and balding,
telling them,
"Kill all Jews—
look what they did to the kid,
kill all Jews,"
and all the epithets that go along with it,
"Heil Hitler" and all of it.
They stabbed him,
which later on the stab wounds were fatal
and he passed away in the hospital.
The Mayor,
hearing about the Cato kid,
came to the Kings County Hospital
to give condolences to the family of the child who had
    regrettably been killed.
At the meantime they had already wheeled in
Mr. Rosenbaum.
He was in the emergency room
and I was at the hospital at the same time,
and the Mayor, seeing me there,
expressed his concern
that a child,
uh, innocent child, had been killed.
Where I explained to him
the fact
that,
whereas the child was killed from an unfortunate accident
where there was no malicious intent,

here
there was an individual lying in the emergency room
who had been stabbed with malicious intent
and for the sole reason—
not that he did anything to anyone—
just from the fact that he happened to be Jewish.
And the mayor went with me to the emergency room
to visit Mr. Rosenbaum.
This was approximately one and a half hours before he
    passed away.
I noticed at the time that his feet
were
completely white.
And I complained to the doctor
on the scene,
"He's having a problem with blood circulation
because there's no blood in his feet."
And she gave me some asinine answer.
And the mayor asked her what his condition is:
"Serious but stable."
In the meantime he was screaming and in pain
and they weren't doing anything.
Subsequently they, um,
they started giving him anaesthesia in a time that
they weren't allowed to give him anaesthesia
and while he was under anaesthesia,
he passed away.
So there was totally mismanagement in his case.
So whereas the Mayor,
had been fed . . .

his people got

whatever information he got out of the Black community was
that

the driver had run a red light

and also,

and that the ambulance,

the Hasidic ambulance,

refused to take care of the Black child that was dying and
rather took care of their own.

Nenh?

And this is what was fed amongst the Black community.

And it was false,

it was totally false

and it was done maliciously

only with the intent to get the riots,

to start up the resulting riots.

The Reverend Canon Doctor Heron Sam Mexican Standoff

(November 12, 1991, 4:00 P.M. The rectory office at St. Mark's Church in Crown Heights. A small, short office. Lived in but impeccably ordered. Some light from lamps, some from overhead. Plaques and awards everywhere. The reverend is wearing a yellow shirt, priest's collar, tan summer jacket. He wears spectacles. There are clocks that make noise and sound the hour in his office and outside church bells sound during the interview, loud. Throughout the talk he is trying to get the corner of a calendar to stay down, but it continues to stick up. Finally he uses a paperweight to keep it down.)

You can't have that kind of accident
if people are observing the speed limits.
People knew it was the Grand Rebbe.
People have seen the Grand Rebbe
charging through the community.
He is worried
about a threat on his life
from the Satmars.
These Lubavitcher people
are really very,
uh, enigmatic people.
They move so easily between
simplicity and sophistication.
Because
they fear for his life,
because the Satmars
who are their sworn enemies

(He laughs/chuckles)
have threatened to *kill*
the Rebbe.
So whenever he comes out
he's gotta be *whisked!*
You know like a President
or even better than a President.
He says he's an intuhnational figuh
like a Pope!
I say
then, "Why don't you get the Swiss guards
to escort you
rather than using the police
and taxpayers' money?"
He's gotta be
whisked!
Quickly through the neighborhood.
Can't walk around.
He used to walk.
When I first came here.
Now he doesn't walk at all.
They drive him.
And when he walked
you could tell he was in front
because there was,
he was protected all around
and they spilled out onto the streets
and buses had to stop
because this BIG BAND
had to escort

the Rebbe from his house over there
to the synagogue.
So the Rebbe goes to the cemetery.
Every time the Rebbe goes to the cemetery,
which is once a week
to visit his wife—dead wife—
and father-in-law,
the police
lead him in escort
charging down the street
at seventy miles an hour in a metropolis—
what do you want?
(Swift increase in volume and suddenly businesslike)
It happened that on this occasion that as they were coming
    back,
uh,
the police car
with its siren,
had gone over a main
intersection with the light
in favor
of the police car.
The Rebbe's Cadillac had passed
when the lights had become amber
and nobody expected the bodyguard van,
uh,
station wagon
to deliberately go through the red light.
So the traffic
that had the right of way kept coming and

BANG!
came the collision and the careening
onto the sidewalk
had to damage whoever was there
and then, um, they were more concerned about licking
    their own
wounds.
Rather than pick
the car off the boy
who died as a result.
And then the ambulance that came—
the Jewish ambulance—
was concerned about the people in the van
while some boy lay dead,
a black boy lay dead on the street.
The people showed their anger,
(Increase in volume)
they burned and whatever else,
upturned
police cars
and looted,
and as a result,
I think in retaliation, murdered one of the Hasidics.
But that was just the match that lit the powder keg.
It's gonna happen again and again.
There's a Mexican standoff right now
But it's gonna happen again.

Anonymous Young Man #1 Wa Wa Wa

(7:00 or 8:00 P.M. Spring. A recreation room at Ebbets Field apartments. A very handsome young Caribbean American man with dreadlocks, in his late teens or early twenties, wearing a bright, loose-fitting shirt. The room is ill equipped. There are a few pieces of broken furniture. It is poorly lit. A woman, Kym, with dreadlocks and shells in her hair, is at the interview. It was originally scheduled to be her interview. The Anonymous Young Man #1 and the other Anonymous Young Man, #2, started by watching the interview from the side of the room but soon approached me and began to join in. Anonymous Young Man #1 was the most vocal. Anonymous Young Man #2 stood lurking in the shadows. A third young man, younger than both of them, wearing wire spectacles and a blue Windbreaker, who looks quite like a young Spike Lee, sat silent with his hands and head on the table the entire time. There is a very bad radio or tape recorder playing music in the background.)

What I saw was
she was pushin'
her brother on the bike like
this,
right?
She was pushin'
him
and he kept dippin' around
like he didn't know how
to ride the bike.
So she kept runnin'
and pushin' him to the side.

So she was already runnin'
when the car was comin'.
So I don't know if she was runnin' towards him
because we was watchin' the car
weavin',
and we was goin'
"Oh, yo
it's a Jew man.
He broke the stop light, they never get arrested."
At first we was laughin', man, we was like
you see they do anything
and get away with it,
and then
we saw that he was out of control,
and den
we started regrettin' laughin',
because then
we saw where he was goin'.
First he hit a car, right,
the tore a whole front fender off a car,
and then we was like
Oh
my god,
man, look at the kids,
you know,
so we was already runnin' over there
by the time the accident happened.
That's how we know he was drinkin'
cause he was like
Wa Wa Wa Wa

Anna Deavere Smith

and I was like
"Yo, man, he's drunk.
Grab him,
grab him.
Don't let him go anywhere."
I said,
"Grab him."
I didn't want him to limp off
in some apartment somewhere
and come back in a different black jacket.
So I was like,
"Grab him,"
and then I was like, "Is the ambulance comin' for the kids?"
'Cause I been in a lot of confrontations with Jews before
and I know that when they said an ambulance
is comin'
it most likely meant for them.
And they was like,
"oh, oh."
Jews right?
"Ambulance comin', ambulance coming',
calm down, calm down,
God will help them,
God will help them if you believe."
And he was actin' like he was dyin'.
"Wa Aww,
me too,
I'm hurt, I'm hurt, I'm hurt too."
Wan nothin wrong with him,
wan nothin wrong with him.

They say that we beat up on that man
that he had to have stitches because of us.
You don't come out of an accident like that unmarked,
without a scratch.
The most he got from us was slapped
by a little kid.
And here come the ambulance
and I was like, "That's not a city ambulance,"
not like this I was upset right
and I was like,
"YO,
the man is drunk!
He ran a red light!
Y'all ain't gonna do nothin'."
Everbody started comin' around, right,
'cause I was talkin' about
these kids is dyin' man!
I'm talkin' about the skull of the baby is on the ground man!
and he's walkin'!
I was like, "Don't let him get into that ambulance!"

And the Jews,
the Jews
was like private, private ambulance
I was like, "Grab him,"
but my buddies was like,
"We can't touch them."
Nobody wanted to grab him,
nobody wanted to touch him,
An' I was breakin' fool, man,
I was goin' mad,
I couldn't believe it.
Everybody just stood
there,
and that made me cry.
I was cryin'
so I left, I went home and watched the rest of it on TV,
it was too lackadazee
so it was like me, man, instigatin' the whole thing.
I got arrested for it
long after
in Queens.
Can't tell you no more about that,
you know.
Hey, wait a minute,
they got eyes and ears everywhere.
What color is the Israeli flag?
And what color are the police cars?
The man was *drunk*,
I open up his car door,
I was like, when—

I was like, he'd been drinkin'
I know our words don't have no meanin',
as Black people in Crown Heights.
You realize, man,
ain't no justice,
aint' never been no justice,
ain't never gonna be no justice.

Michael S. Miller
"Heil Hitler"

(A large airy office in Manhattan on Lexington in the fifties.
Mr. Miller sits behind a big desk in a high-backed swivel
chair drinking coffee. He's wearing a yarmulke. Plays with
the swizzle stick throughout. There is an intercom in the
office, so that when the receptionist calls him, you can
hear it, and when she calls others in other offices, you can
hear it, like a page in a public place, faintly.)

I was at Gavin Cato's funeral,

at nearly every public event

that was conducted by the Lubavitcher community and
   the Jewish

community as a whole

words of comfort

were offered to the family of Gavin Cato.

I can show you a letter that we sent

to the Cato family expressing, uh,

our sorrow over the loss,

unnecessary loss, of their son.

I am not aware of a word

that was spoken at that funeral.

I am not aware of a—

and I was taking notes—

of a word that was uttered

of comfort to the family of Yankele Rosenbaum.

Frankly this was a political rally rather than a funeral.

The individuals you mentioned—

and again,

I am not going to participate in verbal acrimony,
not only
were there cries of, "Kill the Jews"
or,
"Kill the Jew,"
there were cries of, "Heil Hitler."
There were cries of, "Hitler didn't finish the job."
There were cries of,
"Throw them back into the ovens again."
To hear in *Crown Heights*—
and Hitler was no lover of Blacks—
"Heil Hitler"?
"Hitler didn't finish the job"?
"We should heat up the ovens"?
From *Blacks?*
Is more inexplicable
or unexplainable
or any other word that I cannot fathom.
The hatred is so
deep seated
and the hatred
knows no boundaries.
There is no boundary
to anti-Judaism.
The anti-*Judaism*—
if people don't want me
to use,
hear me use the word anti-Semitism.
And I'll be damned if,
if preferential treatment is gonna

be the excuse
for every bottle,
rock,
or pellet that's, uh, directed
toward a Jew
or the window of a Jewish home
or a Jewish store.
And, frankly,
I think the response of the Lubavitcher community was
    relatively
passive.

Henry Rice Knew How to Use Certain Words

(Thursday, November 21, 1991. The Jackson Hole restaurant on Lexington Avenue in the thirties in Manhattan. Lunchtime, dimly lit, a reddish haze on everything, perhaps from a neon light. Mr. Rice, very neatly dressed, is eating a large, messy hamburger and horizontally chopped pickles. Drinking a Miller Lite. Beer is in a bottle next to a red plastic glass. He's wearing a baseball cap over very closely cut hair and a bright, multicolored, expensive-looking colored nylon jacket. Heavy new Timberland boots. Struggling to eat without making a mess of the food. At some point sits up from food and has his right hand or fist on his hip—a very unaffected but truly authoritative stance. Good-natured, handsome, healthy. Patsy Cline's "Crazy" is very loud on the jukebox.)

I went back home and got my bike
because I knew I would have to be
illusive.
I was there in body and in spirit
but I didn't participate in any of the violence
because basically I have a lot to lose.
But I was there
and I would have defended myself if it was necessary,
most definitely.
I weaved around trouble.
When something broke out, I moved back,
when it calmed down, I would move back in on the front line.
I was always there.
And Richard Green heard me saying something to a bunch
   of kids

Anna Deavere Smith

about *voting*
about the power of *vote*
the power of *numbers*
and he said,
uh,
I said, "Get away from me, you're an Uncle Tom,
get away from me.
Get back in your Mercedes-Benz!"
No! I said that to Clarence Norman
and to Richard Green,
both of them.
I was tearing them apart.
Richard Green was very persistent.
He said,
"Look, Mr. Rice,
I like the way you speak.
I need you.
Please help me.
I'm a community activist. . . .
ba, ba, ba, ba, ba."
(He drops some food on his clothes, or so it seems, he
looks and grins)
It didn't get on me.
"I'm a community activist.
I need your help,
please help me,"
and so forth.
Again,
I didn't pay him no mind
but we spoke

some
the next day after that,
after the incidents that took place on that corner
of Albany Avenue.
A brother was beat up—
cops rushing into the Black crowd
didn't rush into the Jewish crowd,
cops rushed into the Black crowd
started beatin' up
Black people.
But the next day Richard came by in a yellow van,
a New York City Department of Transportation van,
with a megaphone,
yellow light flashing,
(Music segues from Patsy Cline's "Crazy" to Public Enemy's
"Can't Truss It," or Naughty by Nature's "O.P.P.")
the whole works
and, um,
he said,
"Henry, I need you in this van.
Drive around with me.
Let's keep some of these kids off the street tonight."
I said, "Okay."
He said,
"The blood
of Black men are on your hands tonight!"
I said, "Okay."
We drive around in the van,
"Young people stay in the house!
Mothers keep your children in the house,

please."
So I began fillin'
I began feeling like
I had to do it
after he told me that,
"the blood of the Black man"
were on my hands,
you know.
Richard Green sure know how to use certain words.
(He giggles)
I remember reaching Albany Avenue—
kids were being chased by the police.
I jump out with a portable megaphone,
I tell them, "Stop running!
The cops won't chase you!
and they won't hit you!"
The next thing I know,
cop grabs my megaphone hits me in the head with a stick,
handcuffs me,
and takes the megaphone out of my hand.
So I'm like,
"Wait a minute
I'm doing a community service for the mayor's office."
They don't want to hear it.
Matter of fact,
they still have the megaphone 'til this day.
I'm like,
"Richard Green get me
out of this police car, please!"
So a Black captain came by,

thank God,

and he says, "What's goin' on?"

Richard Green explained it to him.

He said, "Let him go."

Get back in the van,

there's another Brother in the van,

starts saying,

"Non violence!"

to the young Brothers.

They begin throwing bottles at the, uh,

at the van.

One guy got so upset

he had a nine-millimeter

fully loaded.

He said, "Get the hell out of this neighborhood!"

I told Richard Green, "Take me on home. Shit!"

The next day

more violence:

fires,

cars being burnt,

stores being broken into,

a perception that Black youth

are going crazy in Crown Heights

like we were angry over

nothing,

understand?

Norman Rosenbaum, My Brother's Blood

(A Sunday afternoon. Spring. Crisp, clear, and windy. Across from City Hall in New York City. Crowds of people, predominantly Lubavitcher, with placards. A rally that was organized by Lubavitcher women. All of the speakers were men, but the women stand close to the stage. Mr. Rosenbaum, an Australian, with a beard, hat, and wearing a pinstripe suit, speaks passionately and loudly from the microphone on a stage with a podium. Behind him is a man in an Australian bush hat with a very large Australian flag which blows dramatically in the wind. It is so windy that Mr. Rosenbaum has to hold his hat to keep it on his head.)

Al do lay achee so achee aylay alo dalmo
My brother's blood cries out from the ground.
Let me make it clear
why I'm here.
In August of 1991,
as you all have heard before today,
my brother was killed in the streets of Crown Heights
for no other reason
than that he was a Jew!
The only miracle was
that my brother was the only victim
who paid for being a Jew with his life.
When my brother was surrounded,
each and every American was surrounded.
When my brother was stabbed four times,
each and every American was stabbed four times
and as my brother bled to death in this city,

Anna Deavere Smith

while the medicos stood by
and let him bleed
to death, it was the gravest of indictments against this
    country.
One person out of twenty gutless individuals
who attacked my brother has been arrested.
I for one am not convinced that it is beyond the ability of
    the New York police
to arrest others.
Let me tell you, Mayor Dinkins,
let me tell you, Commissioner Brown:
I'm here,
I'm not going home,
until there is justice.

Norman Rosenbaum
Sixteen Hours
Difference

(7:00 A.M. Spring. Newark Airport, Departure Gate, Continental Airlines. Mr. Rosenbaum is moments before his flight to LA and then back to Australia. Wearing a pinstripe suit with an Australian fit. Hat. Suitcase. He has sparkling blue eyes with a twinkle, rosy cheeks, and a large smile throughout the interview.)

There's sixteen hours difference between New York and
    Melbourne
and I had just gotten back to my office
and I had a phone call from my wife,
and she said she wanted me to come home straight away
and I sensed the urgency in her voice.
I said, "are you all right?" She said, "Yeah."
I said, "are the children all right, you know the kids?" She
    says, "yeah."
So I'm driving home and I'm thinking, I wonder what's
    the problem now, you know?
We had some carpenters doing some work, I wonder if
    there has been a disaster,
some sort of domestic problem,
and I thought, oh my God, you know, my parents,
I didn't even ask after them,
how insensitive not to even ask after my parents,
and I've got a grandmother eighty-five years old, same
    sort of thing.
So I get home,

I walk in the door,
and a friend of mine was standing there,
close friend,
does the same sort of work as me, he's a barrister and an
    academic,
and he sees me and he says,
"There's got a pro—
uh,
we've got a problem.
There's a problem."
I thought he was talking about a case we were working on
    together,
he says, " 'Z come,
come and sit down."
He goes to me,
"There's been a riot in New York,
been a riot in Crown Heights,
Yankel's been stabbed and he's dead."
And
my brother was the last in the world,
I hadn't even given him a thought.
I mean the fact that my brother
could be attacked
or die,
it just hadn't even entered my mind.
At first I appeared all cool, calm and collected.
I then
started asking questions
like who told you,
how do you know,

are you sure?
I just asked the question,
you know,
are you sure?

Anonymous Young Man #2 Bad Boy

(Evening. Spring. The same recreation room as interview with Anonymous Young Man #1. Young Man #2 is wearing a black jacket over his clothes. He has a gold tooth. He has some dreadlocks, and a very odd-shaped multicolored hat. He is soft-spoken, and has a direct gaze. He seems to be very patient with his explanation.)

That youth,
that sixteen-year-old
didn't murder that Jew.
(Pause)
For one thing,
he played baseball, right?
He was a atha-lete,
right?
A bad boy
does
bad things.
Only a bad boy coulda stabbed the man.
Somebody who
does those type a things,
or who sees
those types a things.
A atha-lete
sees people,
is interested in athletics,
stretchin',

Anna Deavere Smith

exercisin',
goin' to his football games,
or his baseball games.
He's not interested
in stabbin'
people.
So
it's not in his mind
to stab,
to just jump into somethin',
that he has no idea about
and
sta—
and kill a man.
A bad boy,
somebody who's groomed in badness,
or did badness
before,
stabbed the man.
Because I used to be a atha-lete
and I used to be a bad boy,
and when I was a atha-lete,
I was a atha-lete.
All I thought about was atha-lete.
I'm not gonna jeoparsize my athleticism
or my career to do anything
that bad people do.
And when I became a bad boy
I'm not a athalete no more.
I'm a bad boy,

and I'm groomin' myself in things that is bad.
You understand, so
he's a athalete,
he's not a bad boy.
It's a big difference.
Like,
mostly the Black youth in Crown Heights have two things
    to do—
either DJ or be a bad boy, right?
You either
DJ, be a MC, a rapper
or Jamaican rapper,
ragamuffin,
or you be a bad boy,
you sell drugs or you rob people.
What do you do?
I sell drugs.
What do you do?
I rap.
That's how it is in Crown Heights.
I been livin' in Crown Heights mosta my life.
I know for a fact that that youth, that sixteen-year-old,
didn't kill that Jew.
That's between me and my Creator.

Anna Deavere Smith

Sonny Carson
Chords

(Lunchtime. Spring. A fancy restaurant in Brooklyn. Sonny tells me it's where all the judges come for lunch. White linen tablecloths. Light wood walls, lamplight next to the table. Tile floor. He is eating crab cakes. He is dressed in a black turtleneck and a gray jacket. He has on a mud cloth hat. He has an authority stick with him, and it lays on the table. His bodyguard, wearing a black leather jacket, enters in the middle of the interview. Sonny chides him for being late.)

It's going to be a long hot summer.
I'm connected up with the young people all over the country
and there's a thread
leading to an eruption
and Crown Heights began the whole thing.
And the Jews come second to the police
when it comes to feelings of dislike among Black folks.
The police,
the police,
believe me, the police—
I know the police and the police know me
and they turned that whole place into an occupied camp
with the Seventy-first Precinct as the overseers.
And don't think that everything is OK within that precinct
    among those officers
either.
Don't think that,
don't think that.
You know the media has always painted me as the bad
    guy—

that's OK!
I'm a good guy to pick on.
Their viewers don't like me either,
they really don't like me because I *am* the bad guy,
I am the ultimate bad guy
because of my relationship to the young people in the city.
I understand their language.
I respect them as the future.
I speak their language. They don't even engage in long
      dialogue
anymore
just short.
"Words."
It always amazes me
how the city fathers,
the power brokers,
just continue to deny what's happening.
And it is just getting intolerable for me to continue to watch
this small
arrogant
group of people continue to get this kind of preferential
      treatment.
They sit on the school board.
A board of nine
and they have
four members, and their kids don't even go to public
      school.
So that's the kind of arrogance I'm talking about.
I have no reason to be eagerly awaiting the coming
      together of our

people.
They owe me first.
I'm not givin' in just like that,
I don't want it.
You can have it.
Like my grandmother said,
"Help the bear!
If you see me and the bear in a fight,
help the bear—
don't help me,
help the bear."
I don't need any of it from them!
And I'm not gonna advocate any coming together and
    healing of
America
and all that shit.
You kiddin'?
You kiddin'?
Just 'cause I can have the fortune of walking in here
and sitting and talking
and having a drink,
it appear that I have all the same kinds of abilities
of other folks in here.
No, it's not that way.
'Cause tonight
by nighttime it could all change for me.
So I'm always aware of that, and that's what keeps me goin'
today
and each day!
(He eats)

I have
this idea
about a film.
See,
these kids, they got
another kinda rhythm now,
there's a whole new kinda
step that they do.
When I first heard rap
I was sittin' in a huge open kinda stadium,
boys and girls high school field,
and I heard these kids come out and start rappin',
and I'm listening
but it's not really clickin',
but I was mesmerized though.
But it was simontaneous
all around the country
and I said, "Oh shit,"
and everybody I knew who was young was listenin' to it
and I said, "Wow."
Because I have always been involved with young people
and all of a sudden I got it,
I really heard the rhythm,
the chords,
the discord.
There's a whole new sound
that the crackers are tryin' to get, but they can't get it.
I heard it on a television commercial.
One of the most beautiful pieces of art
that I ever witnessed

Anna Deavere Smith

was a play
called
um,
um,
um,
'bout, 'bout the Puerto Rican gang—
no, no, no, no, no—
the Puerto Rican gang,
the musical
that was on Broad—
yeah,
West Side Story—
the answer should be
a musical.

Rabbi Shea Hecht
Ovens

(Morning. Spring. A building on Eastern Parkway. A large room with a very long conference table. There are pictures of Lubavitcher men on the walls. Rabbi Hecht is wearing a shirt, open at the neck. He has several crisp one-dollar bills in his shirt pocket. These are, apparently, dollar bills that the Rebbe has given him. It is the custom that the Rebbe gives out one-dollar bills on Sunday. Rabbi Hecht has a beard. He wears glasses, traditional Hasidic garb, including tsitses (ceremonial fringes that hang over his belt) and a red yamulke with gold trim which is ripped. His daughter comes in frequently to get money from him. He keeps telling her to wait until he is finished. She becomes more and more agitated. His brother also enters frequently to ask him questions, and to tell him he's late.)

What is my goal?
My goal is not
to give anybody a message
that we plan on working things out
by integrating
our two
things.
By a person understanding more of their own religion
they will automatically respect another person.
The respect that my religion teaches me has nothing to do
with understanding you.
See, there's a problem.
If
the ony way I'm going to respect you
is based on how much I understand you,
no matter what it is

in certain circles you're gonna run into problems.
Number one,
we are different,
and we think we should and can be different.
When the Rebbe said to the Mayor
that we were all
one people,
I think
what the Rebbe is talking about is that,
that common denominator that we're all children of God,
    and the
respect we all have to give each other under that banner.
But that does not mean that I have to invite you to my
    house for
dinner,
because I cannot go back to your home for dinner,
because you're not gonna give me kosher food.
And I said,
so, like one Black said,
I'll bring in kosher food.
I said eh-eh.
We can't use your ovens,
we can't use your dishes,
it's, it—
it's not just a question of buying certain food,

it's buying the food,
preparing it a certain way.
We can't use your dishes, we can't use your oven.
The—the higher you go
the more common denominator.
And what the Rebbe was saying,
you as the Mayor
don't get caught up in the differences,
you're—
from your position is—
you have to look at it as one city
and one
human race.
We are all New Yorkers
and therefore I will protect all New Yorkers.
You see
preferential treatment
suggests
that you're giving the person
the police car
not because they need the police car
but because
they are who they are.
You're not gonna
give them the housing
because they
need the housing—
you're giving it because of who they are.
But
just because I'm a Jew

therefore I
shouldn't get the police car.
The question is
a synagogue
that has five thousand Jews
leave
the synagogue
at the same time,
do they have a police car to stop the traffic?
The answer is every—single—synagogue,
temple,
mosque,
in
the
world
stops traffic
when five thousand people have to walk out
at the same time.

Anna Deavere Smith

The Reverend Al Sharpton
Rain

(As before.)

The D.A.
came back with no indictment.
Uh, so then our only course
was to ask for a special prosecutor
which is appointed by the Governor,
who's been hostile,
and to sue civilly.
When we went into civil court
we went to get an order to show cause.
The judge signed it and gave me a deadline of three days.
The driver left the country. . . .
No one even said, "Why would he run?
If he did no wrong."
If you and I were in an accident we'd have to go to civil court.
Why is this man
above the law?
So they said, "He's in Israel."
So I said,
"Well, I'll go to Israel to show best effits."
And the deadline
was,
I had to serve him by Tuesday,
which was Yom Kippur—
that was the judge's decision not mine.

So we went.
Alton Maddox and I
got on a plane,
left Monday night,
landed Tuesday morning,
went and served the American embassy, uh,
so that
if this man had any decency at all
he could come to the American embassy and receive service,
which he has not done to this day.
Come back,
went to court
and showed the judge the receipts,
and the judge said, "You made best effits,
therefore you are now permitted,
by default,
to go ahead
and sue the rabbi or whomever
because you cannot do the driver."
So it wasn't just a media grandstand.
We wanted to show the world
one, this man *ran*

and was *allowed* to run, and, two, we wanted to be able to
    legally go
around him,
to sue the people he was working for so that we can bring
    them into
court and establish *why* and what happened.
And it came out in the paper the other day
that the driver in the other car didn't even have a driver's
    license.
So we're dealing with a *complete* outrage here,
we're dealing with a double standard,
we're dealing with uh, uh, a, a
situation where
Blacks do not have equal protection under the law
and the media is used to castigate us
that merely asked for justice
rather than castigate those that would hit a kid
and walk away like he just stepped on a roach!
Uh,
there also is the media
contention of the young Jewish scholar
that was stabbed that night
and they've even distorted
saying *my words at the funeral.*
I *preached* the funeral.
Uh, [the newspaper said I]
helped to, to, uh, uh,
spark or, or, or, or, or *inspire* or *incite* people to kill him
    [Yankel Rosenbaum]
when he was dead the day before
I came out there.

He was killed the night
that the young man
was killed with the car accident.
I didn't even get a call
from the family
'til eighteen hours later.
So there's a whole media distortion
to protect them [the Lubavitchers].
Nobody is talking about,
"Why
is this guy
in flight?"
If I was a rabbi
(I am a ministuh)
and my driver hit a kid,
I would not let the driver *leave*
and I certainlih would give my condolences,
or anything else I could,
to the family,
I don't care what race they are.
To this minute the Rebbe has never even uttered a word of sympathy
to the family,
not even sent 'em a *card*
a flower or *nothing!*
And he's supposed to be a religious leader.
So it's treating us with absolute contempt
and I don't care how controversial it makes us.
I *won't* tolerate being insulted.
If you piss in my face I'm gonna call it *piss*.
I'm not gonna call it rain.

Richard Green
Rage

(2:00 P.M. in a big red van. Green is in the front. He has a driver. I am in the back. Green wears a large knit hat with reggae colors over long dreadlocks. Driving from Crown Heights to Brooklyn College. He turns sideways to face me in the back, and bends down, talking with his elbow on his knee.)

Sharpton, Carson, and Reverend Herbert Daughtry
didn't have any power out there really.
The media gave them power.
But they weren't turning those youfs on and off.
Nobody knew who controlled the switch out there.
Those young people had rage like an oil-well fire
that has to burn out.
All they were doin' was sort of orchestratin' it.
Uh, they were not really the ones that were saying, "Well
stop, go, don't go, stop, turn around, go up."
It wasn't like that.
Those young people had rage out there,
that didn't matter who was in control of that—
that rage had to get out

and that rage
has been building up.
When all those guys have come and gone,
that rage is still out here.
I can show you that rage every day
right up and down this avenue.
We see, sometimes in one month, we see three bodies
in one month. That's rage,
and that's something that nobody has control of.
And I don't know who told you that it was preferential
    treatment for
Blacks that the Mayor kept the cops back. . . .
If the Mayor had turned those cops on?
We would still be in a middle of a battle.
And
I pray on both sides of the fence,
and I tell the people in the Jewish community the same thing,
"This is not something that force will hold."

Those youfs were running on cops without nothing in their
     hands,
seven- and eight- and nine- and ten-year-old boys were
     running at
those cops
with nothing,
just running at 'em.
That's rage.
Those young people out there are angry
and that anger has to be vented,
it has to be negotiated.
And they're not angry at the Lubavitcher community
they're just as angry at you and me,
if it comes to that.
They have no
role models,
no guidance

so they're just out there growin' up on their own,
their peers are their role models,
their peers is who teach them how to move
so when they see the Lubavitchers
they don't know the difference between "Heil Hitler"
and, uh, and uh, whatever else.
They don't know the difference.
When you ask 'em to say who Hitler was they wouldn't
    even be able
to tell you.
Half of them don't even know.
Three quarters of them don't even know.
(Phone rings, Richard picks it up, it's a mobile phone)
"Richard Green, can I help?
Aw, man I tol' you I want some color
up on that wall. Give me some colors.
Look, I'm in the middle of somethin'."
(He returns to the conversation)
Half them don't even know three quarters of 'em.

Just as much as they don't know who Frederick Douglass
    was.
They know Malcolm
because Malcolm has been played up to such an extent now
that they know Malcolm.
But ask who Nat Turner was or Mary McCleod Bethune or
    Booker T.
Because the system has given 'em
Malcolm is convenient and
Spike is goin' to give 'em Malcolm even more.
It's convenient.

Roslyn Malamud
The Coup

(Spring. Midafternoon. The sunny kitchen of a huge, beautiful house on Eastern Parkway in Crown Heights. It's a
large, very well-equipped kitchen. We are sitting at a table
in a breakfast nook area, which is separated by shelves
from the cooking area. There is a window to the side.
There are newspapers on the chair at the far side of the
table. Mrs. Malamud offers me food at the beginning of
the interview. We are drinking coffee. She is wearing a
sweatshirt with a large sequined cat. Her tennis shoes
have matching sequined cats. She has on a black skirt
and is wearing a wig. Her nails are manicured. She has
beautiful eyes that sparkle are very warm, and a very resonant voice. There is a lot of humor in her face.)

Do you know what happened in August here?

You see when you read the newspapers.

I mean my son filmed what was going on,

but when you read the newspapers . . .

Of course I was here

I couldn't leave my house.

I only would go out early during the day.

The police were barricading here.

You see,

I wish

I could just like

go on television.

I wanna scream to the whole world.

They said

that the Blacks were rioting against the Jews in Crown
    Heights

and that the Jews were fighting back.
Do you know that the Blacks who came here to riot were
    not my
neighbors?
I don't love my neighbors.
I don't know my Black neighbors.
There's one lady on President Street—
Claire—
I adore her.
She's my girl friend's next-door neighbor.
I've had a manicure
done in her house and we sit and kibbitz
and stuff
but I don't know them.
I told you we don't mingle socially
because of the difference
of food
and religion
and what have you here.
But
the people in this community
want exactly
what I want out of life.
They want to live
in nice homes.
They all go to work.
They couldn't possibly
have houses here
if they didn't
generally— They have

two,
um,
incomes
that come in.
They want to send their kids to college.
They wanna live a nice quiet life.
They wanna shop for their groceries and cook their meals
    and go to
their Sunday picnics!
They just want to have decent homes and decent lives!
The people who came to riot here
were brought here
by this famous
Reverend Al Sharpton,
which I'd like to know who ordained him?
He brought in a bunch of kids
who didn't have jobs in
the summertime.
I wish you could see the *New York Times*,
unfortunately it was on page twenty,
I mean, they interviewed
one of the Black girls on Utica Avenue.

She said,
"The guys will make you pregnant
at night
and in the morning not know who you are."
(Almost whispering)
And if you're sitting on a front stoop and it's very, very hot
and you have no money
and you have nothing to do with your time
and someone says, "Come on, you wanna riot?"
You know how kids are.
The fault lies with the police department.
The police department did nothing to stop them.
I was sitting here in the front of the house
when bottles were being thrown
and the sergeant tells five hundred policemen
with clubs and helmets and guns
to duck.
And I said to him,
"You're telling them to duck?
What should I do?
I don't have a club and a gun."
Had they put it—
stopped it on the first night
this kid who came from Australia . . .
(She sucks her teeth)
You know,
his parents were Holocaust survivors, he didn't have to die.
He worked,
did a lot of research in Holocaust studies.
He didn't have to die.

What happened on Utica Avenue
was an accident.
JEWISH PEOPLE
DO NOT DRIVE VANS INTO SEVEN-YEAR-OLD BOYS.
YOU WANT TO KNOW SOMETHING? BLACK PEOPLE
 DO NOT DRIVE
VANS INTO SEVEN-YEAR-OLD BOYS.
HISPANIC PEOPLE DON'T DRIVE VANS INTO
 SEVEN-YEAR-OLD BOYS.
IT'S JUST NOT DONE.
PEOPLE LIKE JEFFREY DAHMER MAYBE THEY DO IT.
BUT AVERAGE CITIZENS DO NOT GO OUT AND TRY
 TO KILL
(Sounds like a laugh but it's just a sound)
SEVEN-YEAR-OLD BOYS.
 It was an accident!
But it was allowed to fester and to steam and all that.
When you come here do you see anything that's going on,
 riots?
No.
But Al Sharpton and the likes of him like *Dowerty*,
who by the way has been in prison
and all of a sudden he became Reverend *Dowerty*—
they once did an exposé on him—
but
these guys live off of this,
you understand?
People are not gonna give them money,
contribute to their causes
unless they're out there rabble-rousing.

My Black neighbors?

I mean I spoke to them.

They were hiding in their houses just like I was.

We were scared.

I was scared!

I was really frightened.

I had five hundred policemen standing in front of my house every day

I had mounted police,

but I couldn't leave my block,

because when it got dark I couldn't come back in.

I couldn't meet anyone for dinner.

Thank God, I told you my children were all out of town.

My son was in Russia.

The coup

was exactly the same day as the riot

and I was very upset about it.

He was in Russia running a summer camp

and I was very concerned when I had heard about that.

I hadn't heard from him

that night the riot started.

When I did hear from him I told him to stay in Russia,
    he'd be safer
there than here.
And he was.

        Anna Deavere Smith

Reuven Ostrov
Pogroms

(9:00 P.M. November 1991. In a basement of a Crown Heights house. Mr. Ostrov wears a yamulke. Eating popcorn and sliced apples. Very low, gentle-sounding *nigunim* music plays in the background, it almost sounds like New Age music, perhaps because traditional music is played on a modern electronic keyboard instrument. In the show, I wore a basketball jacket with project CURE's insignia, which Mr. Ostrov did not do at this interview, but previously had at a basketball game. He is clean-shaven, which is unusual for a a Lubavitcher man his age. He had chosen to shave his beard. He has a very rich, deep voice.)

I was working in a hospital.
I work as an assistant chaplain at
Down State Kings County Hospital.
I heard that Yankel Rosenbaum was stabbed and, um, they
were gonna give him an *aurtopsy*
and they asked if he had an
aurtopsy
or not because in the Jewish religion a person is not
    allowed to have
an aurtopsy
and I found out later that he did have one
a few days later.
I found a Jewish man in a room,
a Russian man.
His mother committed suicide
because she was, uhm, she was terrified.
She jumped out of the third floor of her apartment
    building,

committed suicide.
The mother originally came from Russia.
I was speaking to her son
in one of the rooms near the morgue
trying to get his mother not to have an aurtopsy
and he was telling me that the mother
came from Russia eleven years ago
and the mother left Russia eleven years ago
because of the hardships that they had over there,
and when they came to America
and when this thing started to happen in Crown Heights.
It became painful
and it felt like, like there was no place to go.
It's like you're trapped,
everywhere you go there's Jew haters.
And then he told me she commit suicide,
told me the next morning he woke up
he heard the doorbell ring.
He wasn't,
she wasn't there.
He noticed that the window was open,
which is never open
because she was afraid of the cold
even in the summertime.
And he saw his mother
with blood all over her
landed head first
on the concrete side of the apartment building.
After that we already knew this was getting serious,
because we had,

we had Sonny Carson come down
and we had, um,
Reverend Al Sharpton come down
start making pogroms.

Carmel Cato
Lingering

(7:00 P.M. The corner where the accident occurred in Crown Heights. An altar to Gavin is against the wall where the car crashed. Many pieces of cloth are draped. Some writing in color is on the wall. Candle wax is everywhere. There is a rope around the area. Cato is wearing a trench coat, pulled around him. He stands very close to me. Dark outside. Reggae music is in the background. Lights come from stores on each corner. Busy intersection. Sounds from outside. Traffic. Stores open. People in and out of shops. Sounds from inside apartments, televisions, voices, cooking, etc. He speaks in a pronounced West Indian accent.)

In the meanwhile
it was two.
Angela was on the ground
but she was trying to move. Gavin was still.
They was trying to pound him.
I was the father.
I was 'it, chucked, and pushed,
and a lot of
sarcastic words were passed towards me
from the police
while I was trying to explain: It was my kid!
These are my children.
The child was hit you know.
I saw everything, everything,
the guy radiator burst
all the hoses,
the steam,

all the garbage buckets goin' along the building.
And it was very loud,
everything burst.
It's like an atomic bomb,
That's why all these people
comin' round
wanna know what's happening.
Oh it was very outrageous.
Numerous numbers.
All the time the police sayin'
you can't get in,
you can't pass,
and the children laying on the ground.
He was hit at exactly eight-thirty.
Why?
I was standing over there.
There was a little child—
a friend of mine
came up with a little child—
and I lift the child up
and she look at her watch at the same time
and she say it was eight-thirty.
I gave the child back to her.
And then it happen.
Um, Um . . .
My child, these are the things I never dream about.
I take care of my children.
You know it's a funny thing,
if a child get sick and he dies
it won't hurt me so bad,

or if a child run out into the street and get hit down,
it wouldn't hurt me.
That's what's hurtin' me.
The whole week
before Gavin died
my body was changing,
I was having different feelings.
I stop eating,
I didn't et
nothin',
only drink water,
for two weeks;
and I was very touchy—
any least thing that drop
or any song I hear
it would effect me.
Every time I try to do something
I would have to stop.
I was
lingering, lingering, lingering, lingering,
all the time.
But I can do things,
I can see things,
I know that for a fact.
I was telling myself,
"Something is wrong somewhere,"
but I didn't want to see,
I didn't want to accept,
and it was inside of me,
and even when I go home I tell my friends,

"Something coming I could feel it
but I didn't want to see,"
and all the time I just deny deny deny,
and I never thought it was Gavin,
but I didn't have a clue.
I thought it was one of the other children—
the bigger boys
or the girl,
because she worry me,
she won't et—
but Gavin 'ee was 'ealtee,
and he don't cause no trouble.
That's what's devastating me now.
Sometime it make me feel like it's no justice,
like, uh,
the Jewish people,
they are very high up,
it's a very big thing,
they runnin' the whole show
from the judge right down.
And something I don't understand:
The Jewish people, they told me
there are certain people I cannot be seen with
and certain things I can not say
and certain people I can not talk to.
They made that very clear to me—the Jewish people—
they can throw the case out
unless
I go to them with pity.
I don't know what they talkin' about.

Anna Deavere Smith

So I don't know what kind of crap is that.
And make me say things I don't wanna say
and make me do things I don't wanna do.
I am a special person.
I was born different.
I'm a man born by my foot.
I born by my foot.
Anytime a baby comin' by the foot
they either cut the mother
or the baby dies.
But I was born with my foot.
I'm one of the special.
There's no way they can overpower me.
No there's nothing to hide,
you can repeat every word I say.

Photo Credits

Title page, photo by Nancy Siesel/NYT Pictures.

pp. 2, 6, 11, 34, 53, 89, 95, 108, photos by William Gibson/Martha Swope Photography, Inc.

pp. 20, 26, 60, 78, 130, 134, photos by Adger W. Cowans.

p. lii, photo by Bruce H. Savadow.

p. 64, photo by Kathryn Kirk, Office of Howard Golden, President, Borough of Brooklyn.

pp. 65, 118, photos by Ricky Flores.

p. 24, photo by Bill Aron.

p. 133, photo by Andy Uzzle.

pp. 110, 128, photos by Jon Naso/*New York Newsday*.

p. 69, photo by John Paraskevas/*New York Newsday*.

p. 117, photo by Jim Hughes/*New York Daily News* Photo.

p. 132, photo by Helayne Seidman.

p. 124, photo by Kevin Cohen/*New York Post*.

pp. 82, 119, 120, photos by Linda Rosier.

pp. xlviii, l, photos by Clark Jones, Impact Visuals.

pp. 114, 127, photos by Brian Palmer.

Anna Deavere Smith

is an actress and playwright, and Associate Professor of Drama at Stanford University. *Fires in the Mirror* was awarded a Special Citation Obie and was a finalist for the Pulitzer Prize in Drama. Ms. Smith is the recipient of the George and Elizabeth Marton Award, a Lucille Lortel Award for Outstanding Performance by an Actress, a Drama Logue Award, and a Drama Desk Award.

Cornel West

is Director of Afro-American Studies at Princeton University and author of several books, including, most recently, *Race Matters*.